"Wherever You Go, There You Are" – © Buddha

Personal stories and such by John Boland

(nonfiction)

Dedicated to Babaji and Krista for their inspiration at the 'perfect moment'

johnboland.com

I discovered that my favourite illustrator
W. Heath Robinson's work entered the public domain
in 2015
So I thought I'd throw this in, given that I'm writing this
page during the pandemic. I love the Title :

THE ANNUAL DANCE GIVEN TO SPIRITUAL
MEDIUMS BY
THE PSYCHOLOGICAL SOCIETY
DANCING WITH SPIRITUAL PARTNERS TO
SPIRITUAL MUSIC PLAYED BY SPIRITUAL
INSTRUMENTS

THE ANNUAL DANCE GIVEN TO SPIRIT MEDIUMS BY THE PSYCHOLOGICAL SOCIETY

DANCING WITH SPIRITUAL PARTNERS TO SPIRITUAL MUSIC PLAYED BY SPIRITUAL INSTRUMENTS

"Wherever you go, there you are" – © Buddha

These stories are true. They were written in anticipation of publishing in a new Canadian magazine. However, the publisher left so the chance evaporated. Besides, the magazine hoped to depend on ads for cannabis related products. According to the laws in Canada that accompanied what is falsely called 'legalization' of cannabis, ads for cannabis etc. are illegal. Since these stories were written and edited to be about 350 words to fit the magazine space, I subsequently redid them slightly, enjoying the freedom to not stick to such a rigid format.

They are more or less in order of time written as that was how my memories appeared. Why bother messing with that? ahaha...

Each story has a trigger alert. Some are serious, some humorous. Each story has a link to a song on youtube that I felt was somehow appropriate to the subject. No violation of any copyright is intended and any such possible violation is surely the responsibility of youtube/poster on youtube. If you enjoy the songs, I encourage you to buy them from a site such as itunes or purchase Spotify. The Kindle ebook version has youtube links to all the songs listed. However, I have deleted the links for the Paperback version and just left the song title so they can be looked up.

Disclaimer (General) :
The magazine was going to call me 'Happy Pappy' as that is a nickname my daughter uses. So the name remains in some of the stories. It is not associated with any other people or characters called 'happy pappy'.

DO NOT try these in real or unreal life. They are mostly historical and the world now seems much more unsafe. Happy Pappy wants you safe. But basically, if your life is somehow influenced by reading these stories, please do not blame me and more importantly do NOT sue Happy Pappy or anyone foolish enough to publish them. Besides, Happy Pappy remains an enigmatic hobo so has no money.

Note 1 : some stories are better soon after the legal consumption of a cannabis substance. You must be of legal age (Canada) or legal wherever you live.

Note 2 : (repeated for emphasis due to fear) - the music title links go to youtube in the Kindle ebook version. No copyright infringements are intended since any infringements are the responsibility of the person posting on youtube.

Most of the music is also available on Spotify or itunes.

Note 3 : In reality, some trigger warnings are important in life especially for abuse survivors and people with PTSD. Here, the trigger warnings and phobias are in jest unless noted. Since the stories were meant to be published periodically, the trigger warnings/phobias would have seemed less repetitive, annoying. Just enjoy the ride and take care.

"Everybody is playing with their stories; who they think they are. It's more fun to just witness it all. To be in the environment in which it's all happening." Ram Dass

Amsterdam to Morocco – hitchhiking (a snippet)

Suggested Music : Already Gone by The Eagles (live NYC 1994)
Trigger Alert: Those with hodophobia (fear of travelling) may want to stop reading.

This is not about one of those great but expensive train passes through Europe. Nope. It's a snippet of how to not hitchhike to Morocco from Amsterdam. I had left a girlfriend behind since she was screwing somebody else. Admittedly he was handsome but had also inherited 26 million dollars. He eventually dumped her. This story was due to be published in a new mag but that fell through. It would have been published where she lives. I was hoping she'd come across it. It's not mean though I certainly felt that way before leaving. I still love her but was sure she'd see the pain. Passive aggressive distant love for Eileen, I actually think she'd laugh at that ... But now to the story.

I love Amsterdam but will skip that part as it's a bit of a blur and if it comes back sometime, maybe I can write it down. Let's skip all the rides to get to Paris. Now in terms of sleeping, one would think I'd remember a hostel in Paris. No. Those long-term memory cells must also be in the fried category.
(Happy Pappy helpful hints – if you repeat something 8 times, it goes into your long-term memory. Helps with such things as

people's names. Now practice by saying Happy Pappy 8 times...see...you feel better. Right ? ...)

I do remember taking a detour to avoid Marseilles as at the time, I was told it was a dock city known for heroin smuggling. (I'm sure it is now a lovely place with a great tourist bureau). I ended up in a tiny French village where tourists never went. The only hotel had their prices listed on the wall. I don't know what the 50 franc room looked like but on the bottom in small letters it had a 10 franc room. Turned out it was the tiny attic of the old building. Perfect view of the town square made it one of my favourite hotels. I spent hours watching people in the square, coming and going. The local wine for cheap helped as well. Also, conveniently located near a tiny rail line through the mountains to Spain. I'd give the hotel 5 stars on trip advisor. If I could remember the name of the place...if I'd said it 8 times.

Places not to sleep

Spanish jails

Two days out of Barcelona, hitchhiking hadn't been bad or great. I had been with 2 women I met and that made getting a ride easier. But alas they got a ride by themselves and my soon to be desperate situation meant I never caught up so we could meet in Morocco. I was now halfway down the Spanish Gold Coast, still heading to Morocco. It was late in the day as I got let out in a lonely section of country. I could see the clouds were dark, ominous and I could think it was getting dark quickly. I know from sleeping in the ditch by Golden, BC that this is not advisable at all.

A Mercedes (Mercenary Bents) stopped. Two Germans guys in black leather pants. Alarm bells were going off but I ignored them. They stopped at a bar in nowheresville and we drank a lot of cognac. I have to say as much as I like cognac, I never drank it again. I decided that since it was a long all night ride to Morocco, I would take a quaalude. (It seemed that many drugs in Spain were OTC but certainly not weed which at the time was severely enforced). We got going but not for long. The driver guy got out to pee at a pull over but I think he forgot to pee as he came back with a very large gun with what kinda looked like a silencer. They wanted everything. Traveller's checks, passport, cash, my pack. And after all that as I managed to get out of the car, they said it was time to shot me. At that split moment, the aforementioned ditch to sleep in way back there in Golden seemed very desirable...

Women of the Night (Spanish Jails)

Suggested Music : Gotta Get You a Woman by Todd Rundgren

Trigger Alert : Those with cyprianophobia, the fear prostitutes (sex trade workers), may want to stop reading

Recently, I referred to someone as having been a prostitute. They were. I was quickly corrected to 'sex trade worker'. That works too. A monetary or otherwise compensation for having sex.

Well, I survived the robbery. Otherwise I wouldn't be here writing this... They drove off with everything. I somehow got a ride to the local airport as there they spoke English. Recall that I was drunk from cognac with a quaalude chaser but had sobered up instantly. They got me to the police station where they did not speak English but I guess knew I wasn't a criminal. However, now the middle of the night, there was only one place to sleep - the one large cell - are they called cattle cells? My all female cellmates were all quite obviously involved in what I would now refer to as the sex trade. At the time, I would have used non pc words. I liked the women as they treated me very well. I only had my clothes on my back and maybe about 40 cents equivalent in pesetas. But I had cigarettes. I was popular with the smokes. And a blanket. The jail was completely cement and despite rumours, the Costa de Sol is cold in January. If the jail liked you, you got a blanket. So I had the only blanket and gave it to the women who seemed the coldest. Their trade seemed to call for not a lot of clothing. We had a good time laughing though we had no idea about what as we had no words in common. But the good times came to an end in the morning with no cigarettes and no returned 'favours' (read sex acts) from my new found friends. The guards took me outside and pointed me down the street. Were they kicking a hobo out of town with nothing like they had done in Golden? Were they telling me there was something better down the street?

Karma Rising

Suggested Music : Breathe Me by Sia – Live at SxSW (last episode of *Six Feet Under* – no spoilers)
Trigger Alert : Those with fear of karma, keep reading...

Have you been paying attention? There will be a quiz...
So fresh from no sleep at the Spanish jail and headed down the street as pointed by the guards - kicking hobos out of town or...It turned out to be the British Vice Consul Office. Yes, as a Canadian I could use it !!! So I was quickly ushered into to see the Vice Consul. After my short version of robbery, he handed me a wack of cash pesedas and told me the hotel across the way would take care of me. 'Come back tomorrow after food and sleep'. So yes, I did return. He took me back to the jail and introduced me to the Chief of Police (Jefe de Policia) which of course was not his real title as dictator Franco had disbanded all police for just the Army - a typical fascist move. But he spoke perfect Oxford English. I didn't ask how as I think he had a picture of Franco behind him. He took my story down, and told me 'we will catch them, this is Spain'. This was not the first time I had heard a version of 'don't worry, this is Spain...' A somewhat scary hint at what fascism does.
So it took about a month to get a passport from Canada and some wired cash. And that's really fast. And despite never liking beer, my evenings turned into Spanish beer in the local bar

watching Spanish TV and people showing off lottery tickets as a sign of wealth.

I decided to go south to the beaches to await my travellers checks. Remind me to write a story called 'don't leave home without them' in reference to American Express traveller's checks. For now, safe to say I now use Visa checks. I went to thank the Vice Consul who said 'I was just coming to get you. The Jefe of Policia wants to see you.' So last stop before my bus south. Yes bus. The chief handed me a picture and said 'is this one of the robbers'? And indeed it was. 'He is wanted for bank robbery. We will catch him. This is Spain. He will 'go away' and chances of survival in a Spanish prison are slim. This is Spain...' Later I heard about a black Mercedes trying to run a roadblock. Spanish Franco army tended to shoot first and ask questions later. They all have machine guns. The occupants did not survive...I wonder...I hope...

More Places not to Sleep (aka flying cockroaches)

Suggested Music : One Fine Morning by Lighthouse, live 1972 Massey Hall, intro by the late Skip Prokop, vocals by the late Bob McBride

Trigger alert - if you fear cockroaches (Katsaridaphobia) don't read this...

'as god is my witness, i thought cockroaches could NOT fly...' (apologies to WKRP)

Somewhere in Pakistan:

I had a shelter childhood. I'd never seen a cockroach. When I was in University, I heard that some obviously evil people off campus had roaches (both kinds).

I was staying in a slightly lower than acceptable hotel somewhere in Pakistan. Later I lived in Tibetan villages where cockroaches were everywhere since the Tibetans killed nothing. They were all over the walls of your hotel room but never came on the bed or floors so it didn't bother me after a while. But back in Pakistan, I turn off the light in my hotel room and hear a strange noise like a sick Cicada. It was a FLYING cockroach, noisy and big and flying randomly everywhere. I had no idea if he planned on landing on me or any other nefarious deed. When I went to get the 'desk clerk', he clearly thought I was a total wimp but kindly killed it but left it's crushed self on the floor.

Since then, I suffer from (FLYING) Katsaridaphobia. I remember changing hotels in Kathmandu to a more expensive one because, yup, as soon as the light went out, there came the all too familiar sound.

Sleeping in the Ganges

(or at least close to that, you'll see...)

Part 1 (kinda long so pay attention)

Suggested Video : Sunrise Semester with Mort Finkel (SCTV with Harold Ramis) – Note: see Trigger Alert before watching.

Trigger Alert : Those with dentophobia, fear of the dentist, may not want to watch the suggested video and may want to stop reading. This is a serious warning.

My back top molar really hurt. It had hurt in Nepal but two Mandrax took care of that. It hurt even as I passed out from the pills. But not in the morning. But it did return. I was living on a houseboat in Benares (Varanasi) in India. Big enough for 3, one big room with a top deck, toilet was hole in floor but you couldn't beat the price of $3 a month...yup, a month total. Oh also, it was far from the burning (cremation) ghats as Benares is the holy place to get cremated and have your ashes shovelled into the Ganges river. But dead holy men and babies are not burned but put in the river as is. So that could be seen as a drawback cause from the deck one could see the occasional holy man's body float by. But remember the low rent (3 cents a day, each person).

There was a local dentist I found. He was trained in Britain, had the accent. I'm sure he was good but his locale limited his services. He did not have an electric drill but instead had a treadle sewing machine sort of thing. Of course I was hoping his leg did not tire. He filled it ok but the tooth broke in half couple days later. So extraction time. He was not apparently allowed to administer any kind of pain killer outside of homeopathic. This seemed strange of course because there at least in Benares, all drugs were decriminalized - even morphine. Bhang lassis (kinda like a smoothie with cannabis paste) at the corner for a rupee (about 10 cents then). Now sadly I had none of the above painkillers on me so I had it pulled a la carte with a pair of pliers (remember – no anaesthetic). For the first few seconds, it didn't hurt. He had to show me the tooth before I believed him. At that point it hurt. And I mean hurt a lot. I knew the druggist down the street (I'd been there 3 months as I liked the rent and loved Benares). I prayed he would give me a magic pain pill...So I quickly scampered on down there...

I was making my way quickly to the local pharmacy. Given that morphine was over the counter for about 10 cents a hit, the benches out front were occupied by addicts nodding off. There were few overdoses and the druggist measured doses carefully. However, there is nothing quite like a junkie who has used for a long time. They are extremely thin with death in their eyes as their days are numbered.

The druggist knew me though I didn't abuse anything except maybe bhang lassies. No OTC mandrax or anything though I'm sure he had some. He gave me a pill but would not say what it was. 'Wait 30 minutes, if it doesn't work by then, tell me.' So I hung out on the bench with the junkies wondering how to tell time as I did not have a watch (I didn't even have shoes) and clocks did not seem to exist. I didn't have much to do considering that the junkies were nodding off and even if not, talking to 'pending death' did not seem somehow helpful to me at least. So when I thought time was up, which was difficult given the aforementioned excruciating pain, I asked/begged for another pill.

'Here's another one but don't take it for a while as the first one will work soon.' Yup, sure did, about 30 seconds after I immediately left and took the second pill. OOOPS.

The houseboat I lived on (the $3 a month one) was down a long, very narrow alley. This being the main alley. Even so, it was so narrow that if a cow came along, you had to spread eagle against the walls or be crushed. I myself was now bouncing from wall to wall but somehow, I made it to the houseboat gang plank. I made the big drug induced mistake of thinking I could actually 'walk the plank'. Nope. I made it halfway and fell right into the river. My friend on the boat heard me and rescued me. Without that, I would have permanently gone to sleep in the Ganges. I would have been like one of the holy men floating down the river.

Next morning I awoke. Hey, no tooth pain. I sat up and quickly realized that falling off the plank had broken 3 ribs which I had not noticed...But like I said, no tooth pain which has never come back (given that teeth don't grow back...).

In Defense of Denial, (aka) Miso Soup for the Anxious Soul

This is a change of pace before *Sleeping with Tigers*, which is next...When these stories were to be published in a magazine, it seemed a break from strange sleeping places was needed.

Suggested Music : Laughing by the Guess Who (live from 1969)
Trigger Warning (true/real this time) - This jest about denial is not meant to justify in any way denial in incidents of abuse or violence.

Denial, there are many good things about it :
1) it protects you as a child, as let's face it, everyone seems to come from a dysfunctional family, so parents must be very fucked up. So we need to be protected by childhood denial.
2) Denial is way better than lying. First, you don't know it's a lie. Second, it's guilt free. And third, even if you do know it's lying, you can later claim denial on the witness stand.
3) Denial also protects you from other icky feelings such as sadness, loneliness and a third that I'm currently in denial about. The only feeling that might arise is anger and you can easily deny that as in "I'M NOT ANGRY" (*said in loud voice*).
4) You just don't have to take any responsibility. Fault is not yours. (And you can always project that.)
5) Denial can help keep you in a negative state and as you can see later on, this can be a very positive thing.

6) Denial helps keep obsessive thoughts strong so that compulsive behaviour stays in place which keeps depression at bay.

7) Denial is an integral part of depression.

8) If you are a politician or a criminal lawyer, denial is like the mother lode of manna. (I have no idea what mother lode of manna means but it's alliteration at least…)

9) Denial keeps all kinds of therapists, psychologists, and psychiatrists in business and in many places, that has to be the #2 industry after cannabis...

10) and #10 was important but I forget, honest, I forget…

Sleeping with the Tigers

Suggested Music : Hunting Tigers out in India by Bonzo Dog Band (funny)
Trigger Alert : Those with Ailurophobia (fear of cats) may want to stop reading

I was hitchhiking in India from Benares to Puri. Just over 1000 km. Now, at that time, the main road was dirt, one lane and had only trucks. And hitchhiking could mean walking long distances or just waiting at a tea shop for a ride. But I usually got a ride and was also given the 'traditional' gift of a piece of opium to eat. In the long run, not wise at all but certainly expected by the addicted truck drivers. It didn't make them sleepy as in large amounts, it causes a rebound effect of strong wakefulness. Not at all recommended (either way) but especially in large amounts due not only addiction but it can kill you in an overdose.
But I had a big Bartholomew map of India stuffed in my tiny pack that showed a short cut right turn to Puri thereby avoiding Calcutta. At least it looked like a good road. You couldn't tell. I eventually got a ride to a city called Ranchi. It was famous for the Yogananda Ashram, one of the good ones (which I never found). But my ride drove me to the Catholic Monastery as they would put me up. A great dinner and nights sleep and I was up at dawn to keep going. I wanted to be in Puri for Xmas, on the ocean beach. The one thing I didn't know and no one told me was that the short cut road to Puri now what would be best

described as 'petered out'. I think if I had stayed the next morning, the monks would have told me not to keep going. Good advice. It was wide enough for a truck barely but close also to becoming a trail. I wasn't in the mood for turning around so I thought I'd just walk, hope that a truck appeared. I have no recollection of how far I walked. It was warm out but not hot. Hadn't rained in at least 2 or 3 months. I wonder what I did for water? Odd the things one remembers but forgets others.

There was a billboard sign, typical of leftovers from the British. It read 'Future site of ---- wildlife reserve'. I didn't think much beyond the sign being there for a long time and completely crumbling. My guess was that the idea had gone nowhere. Apparently, the animals had not got the meme.

Somewhere down the 'road' was a small sign on the side, really quite small. Not like a deer crossing sign. Way smaller. Coulda easily missed it...

'Tiger Crossing'

I only had 3 choices...turn back, freeze, go forward

1) turn back : I don't like retracing my steps. I like hiking trails that go somewhere new. Besides, don't tigers stock their prey? I didn't want to find out. I didn't even bother to google it right now.

2) freeze: There was certainly no point to waiting to see if the sign was correct.

3) go forward: the only real choice though as I recall my step was a bit spryer. I also recall being in a campsite in BC where bears tended to also live. The sign on the washroom door just said 'Food Runs'. And tigers in the day usually sleep or hang out near a water hole. At least I hoped that was true. At least of Bengal

tigers. And they weren't as rare then as they sadly are now.
Once again I survived or else I wouldn't be Happy Pappy and be writing. I eventually came across a very small village which was for some reason built in a circle. Later I realized that was the best way to guard against a nighttime maundering tiger. The people looked in total shock as either they rarely saw white people or more likely anyone who survived the jaunt through the jungle. I had also not considered Cobras that I read can chase you very quickly. I guess 'Cobra Crossing' signs would be superfluous.

I had a tea at the only chai shop and realized that the villagers were gathering money to buy me a bus ticket through the rest of the jungle. Now this village appeared extremely poor and isolated so to get bus fare together was amazing. I did take the bus and got out at the end of the jungle and kept walking. After all, it was only 1000 kilometers to Puri...Next time, I'll take the bus through the complete jungle.

Remember : Go forward...

Fear of squirrels

Suggested Music : That'll be the Day by Buddy Holly (live on Ed Sullivan)

Trigger Alert : Those with sciurophobia (fear of squirrels) may want to stop reading – HEY !!! That's me...

Someone I know very well lives in Rockland in Victoria, Canada which is an area with many historic homes. BUT they say it's the smallest historic home which maybe is supposed to make it seem less yuppieish. Their neighbours on 2 sides are RCMP in large historic homes - I guess there may be a lesson there.

My friend hates squirrels (the invasive kind) and has water pump type toys that shoot 30 feet. They put ammonia and water in the squirt gun. Squirrels hate ammonia and once hit generally move on.

One day, they saw a squirrel in their yard and quickly went to get the gun, saying to their friend 'I'm going in to get the gun'. They tried but the squirrel was long gone.

Later that day, one of the RCMP neighbours called out to them asking what were they doing earlier on. They decided that in the future they will instead yell out 'I'm going to go get the WATER pistol'...then realized that might not sound that great either if the water part was not heard...Now I think they will be more secretive about their use of water guns...

Presented by the SFZ (Squirrel Free Zones). Please like our facebook page.

My Best post holiday event:

Suggested Music : One on One by Hall and Oates, live at the Troubadour 2008

Trigger Warning : Those with iatrophobia (fear of Doctors) may want to stop reading...

I went to my GP (family doctor). Having one here is like winning the lottery as there are no GPs taking new patients. Period. I think I saw two were listed but one is a quack and the other one is a dead quack. Maybe they should take them off as accepting new patients, unless someone knows something I don't. Maybe therapy is free in the Bardo...

My doctor and I decided my new years resolution will be:'less Eeyore / more Tigger...' So far it's working.

Also read *'Pathology in the Hundred Acre Wood: a neurodevelopmental perspective on A.A. Milne'* by Dr. Sarah E. Shea (et al), Developmental Clinic, IWK Grace Health Centre, Halifax NS – a perfect description of what is wrong with psychiatry sometimes. One would hope the article is in jest or else I would maybe (in jest) need to diagnose the author with Personality Disorder (mixed) with a strong propensity to project...

Reply online from my friend Russ in Berlin :

'add a pinch of piglet'

It was a long way to come see you

Suggested Music : One More Mountain to Climb by Dr. Music
Trigger Alert : Those with hodophobia (fear of travel) may want to stop reading)...I think I used this fear before so perhaps there is an emerging theme. Note how close this is to the word hobophobia...

I'm a professional. Besides the hobo part.
So I was looking for work and saw a job in the Caymans. I was in the process of writing detective fiction about there. So I figured maybe I can get a free trip there, have an interview, pick up a station wagon I knew of in Georgia and see a friend in Maine and stop at my cottage on the way back to BC. Wow. That was a lot of travelling to take care of and I only had 30 days car insurance. But sounded great. Lots of modern hobos have a station wagon or van. Riding the rods is not like it was. Besides there no railways to the Caymans.
No problem, I got the interview, free trip, night at the Hilton and off to Georgia. The interview was kinda strange as it consisted of one man from Canada and some Caymanians. The Caymanians clearly did not want to hire me and the Canadian dude was kinda screwed up... and it was really hot...
The wagon was not quite in as good shape as I hoped. But it drove pretty well. The ownership was a bit shaky, not that I thought it was hot but the plates were from another car and the ownership papers looked a bit dodgy but hey, maybe Georgia

ownerships were like that. Maybe made in private prisons like they used to be here. What did I know. Off to Maine to see my friend who wasn't expecting me and as long as no one ran the plates, I was fine.

Now my friend was a very successful author in Europe but just a cult following in the US. However, he loved Maine and had 40 acres on the ocean. He knew I was going to visit but didn't know when and basically never answered the phone. So I was going to arrive basically unannounced.

Before going there, I ended up spending the night in Bangor, Maine as I had been driving non stop from Georgia and that's a long way. You may not know it but Steven King lives in Bangor and I think always has. I like to stop in Tourist Bureaus as I learn interesting things. In the one in Bangor, they had a pile on the counter of 'maps to Steven King's house'. This really surprised me. I mean, would he want a bunch of tourists showing up? The woman at the Bureau told me that he was a 'Bangor boy' and if you drove to his house and the gates were open, you could knock and he would come out and sign your books. If the gate was closed, well, this wasn't an option. I still find that amazing.

But I was looking for another author. I knew approximately where he lived but it was hard to find. So I went to the first country corner store I could find, bought a variety of Maine micro brews (I still drank then) and asked where my friend Janwillem van de Wetering lived. A customer gave me detailed instructions which turned out to take me way, way out for miles and miles on an ocean spit. I figured that the directions were intentionally wrong. I saw a couple sitting out in their front yard, so I stopped and asked them. They said they had the same domestic help as he did and gave me precise directions. Which of course were all the way back, just past that country store.

I pulled in and everything was fine. He told me that he would occasionally get uninvited guests, particularly Germans as his books were very popular there. He would give them a basketball, play for a few minutes and then leave them there. Eventually they would give up and leave. I told him maybe he could get a gate like Mr. King. He laughed.

We spent the afternoon basically weeding the yard as his young grandson was visiting. He did say if he wasn't so busy that week with his daughter, we would go fishing. Later, I saw pictures of his dock and boat and realized this would have been close to perfection. His wife Juanita was incredible. We went to dinner and then he let me sleep in one of his special little cabins that were built by very talented artisans. All over his property were amazing sculptures that he made from driftwood and seashells. He would do this in manic spurts until they were done. There used to be pictures of them on the web but they seem to have disappeared.

I wanted him to read my first book. He agreed and the next morning, he signed a bunch of his books he had given me. We went to breakfast in Ellsworth, population about 8000. Of course, being Maine, it had a really good cafe. One of his paintings hangs at the entrance. He said:

'I read half your book last night and will finish it tonight.' I hesitated as I asked what he thought. 'I could say one of 3 things: ahhh, ummm, or publish as soon as possible. It's the third.' I

asked if he would introduce me to an agent (he of course had a top agent). 'If you can drive that station wagon from Georgia to here, you can find an agent'. I said 'It's a long way to come see you...'
I realize now that this was a challenge, a mission of sorts. Thank you, Janwillem.

PS : Dear Publishers/Readers : Given that many of these stories were to be published in a national magazine, but are not due to the crazy cannabis laws in Canada, my mission remains...'got an agent and/or publisher?'
PPS : I had planned to take the ferry from Maine so I could go visit an old girlfriend I still love. But the car was acting up...so I never went to Halifax...wish I had, in case she reads this...

Sadly, Janwillem passed into the next Bardo about 2 years after my visit. Soon after, so did his wife Juanita .

Sleeping with mosquitoes

Trigger alerts: if you have entomophobia (also known as insectophobia - fear of specific insects) or thalassophobia (fear of oceans) or hemophobia (fear of blood), you may want to immediately stop reading.

Suggested sounds: see trigger alert...
https://www.youtube.com/watch?v=RWfQ46PM5jo

Some may recall my close encounter with sharks on my beach walk from Puri, India. Or maybe I haven't even added it yet...If so, you really have something to look forward to...

I had eventually ended up down in southern India at a magical place called Mahabalipuram. There are 7 stone temples heading into the ocean. It is said that when all seven are covered by water, then ... well it's not great. There is only one left with waves crashing at its edge. I had been sleeping on the beach when I met some Indian 'hippies' (a very rare being at the time). They lived in a thatched shack up the beach. They invited me to stay there but I think it was probably because I still had half a kilo of Menali hash and they had chillums and matches. Perfect combinations. (note that Menali and the Kulu valley are no longer considered safe).

The first day together, we had been hanging out in the caves and the very famous temple and smoking chillums of course. Just about sunset back in the shack, I heard a noise that sounded like a plane overhead. But I thought 'hey, there's no planes go by here'. Then I found out. It was the sound of many, many thousands of mosquitoes about to attack. I was suddenly covered by them. My arms and legs were basic black and likely soon to be basic red (see trigger alert). When I looked at my hippie roommates, there was not a mosquito near them. If I'd known the expression WTF, I would have said it. My obvious questions to them were 1) what am I to do as they had no netting and 2) why were they not on them too? I figured it wasn't just my WASPY blood.

All they said was 'when you have them for 365 days of the year, you get used to them' and 'you'll have to go sleep on the beach as the ocean breeze blows them away'. Which of course is exactly what I did. I moved back to my own beach and we visited in the day at the caves.

Now when I go to the cottage in Ontario every summer, I tell this story to my guests when they ask why mosquitoes don't come near me...I'm not all sure they believe me but seem to come around the next day when feeling their itchy bites (and I have none)...

Burma Airways

Suggested music : Katmandu by Cat Stevens (yes, he spelt it wrong as he was not in Kathmandu when he wrote it – he was in a London hospital).
Trigger Alert : Those with aviophobia (fear of flying) may want to stop reading.

My friend wanted to fly from Kathmandu to Rangoon, capital of what was then Burma, now called Myanmar. It was the cheapest way to get to Bangkok. You couldn't really stay in Burma as it was mostly a closed country so the plane just stopped briefly and then went to Bangkok.
Myanmar National Airlines used to be called Burma Airways. It no longer flies that route but the cheapest now is about 6 to 7 hundred dollars on other airlines. Burma Airways was at the time considered one of the worst airlines in the world. The joke floating around the restaurants in Kathmandu was that the pilots were smoking Thai stick in bongs.
We went to the Burma Airways office. The clerk said it was $120 to Bangkok one way. My friend (he had been told in a restaurant by another Kathmanduian) to say 'I was told by a friend that he paid $80 with a stay over in Rangoon of maximum 7 days'. (Burma would give you a 7 day, expensive visa, very strongly enforced, even harsher than Nepal where you could play the visa game for 3 months before guaranteed deportation). The clerk said he had to go check. He disappeared behind a curtain. Every

decision in Kathmandu seemed to be made behind a curtain. We joked about the wizard likely behind the curtain. Five minutes went by. Clerk came out and said '89'.

We went to one of the Western food restaurants where joints were fine but chillums not allowed. One of the travellers was saying how he was flying to Thailand on Burma Airways for only $120...We didn't have the heart to say anything beyond 'hey, I'm on the same flight'.

Note: Mynamar Airlines is no longer listed in the top 10 worst airlines. The worst is now listed a WOW Air (now defunct after leaving countless people stranded). So that makes it a toss up for worst airline : Royal Jordanian Airlines and Pakistan International Airlines...take your pick. I know which probably should win the worse. btw, Mynamar is listed in 2022 in list of countries not to visit with Russia now also making the (failing) grade

Happy Pappy Loves NYC

Suggested Music : New York City, You're a Woman by Al Kooper
Trigger Alert : Those with fear of large cities (no phobia name listed on google) may want to stop reading.

I hadn't been there in more than 40 years. I went there at least once a year when I was a child since my wonderful Aunt Dorothy lived there. Hence, I love NYC then and now. Though my fear of tall buildings began there when my father took me up the Empire State Building. This time I was there for a Memorial Service for a friend (Spalding Gray) but even got into Letterman after trying for 3 nights. And Amy Sedaris was the surprise guest - pinch me...

I was stopped on the street a number of times and told that I looked like Gerry Garcia or his brother at least. The first time, I thought of it as a strange compliment that didn't apply beyond my long hair. But I'm not a doppelganger, even close. After I few times being told this by random men on the street, I became somewhat suspicious. I realized that I probably wasn't paranoid to think this must be code. I figured it was either maybe a drug or gay thing. I never found out. But I do love NYC...It was post 9/11 and I was amazed by 2 things. First, people were very friendly. If I stopped to look at my map, at least 3 people almost immediately stopped to help. And second, it was very safe. I think that the large number of police everywhere may have had an impact. I still love NYC...

My friend's doctor

Full disclosure : end of story is made up. Rest is true

Suggested music : Eeyore quotes:

https://www.youtube.com/watch?=7xPnUe6Xcbw

Trigger alert: those with mania

A friend went to see their GP (yes, amazingly, they had a GP which are really hard to find). They had been somewhat depressed but not really catastrophic. They told the doctor. Their doctor told them a story, kinda of a quick Milton Erickson therapy type tale:

"I used to be an emergency department doctor. We had this patient who came in to emerg all the time, often every day. He described being very depressed such that he could not function (note that he could function to get to the emergency almost every day). The staff called him 'Eeyore'. I asked him 'have you ever been in the Third World?' The patient said no."

I said 'You live in the first world, man. Appreciate your good fortune. Get up every morning and write 'I appreciate living in the first world'.

Don't write anything more. This is not a journal. Then get up and do whatever you do in the morning. In the evening, get on your computer. Do not check your email or watch anything else except stream what is called '*Living with Nomads*' with Kate Humble. You can find it free at https://www.knowledge.ca/program/kate-humble-living-nomads. Do you hate hot weather or cold weather the most?

'Cold weather' he said.

'Ok then first watch the episode about Nomads in Siberia and how they live to survive. You can watch other ones too. Like the one in Mongolia or any of the others in her series. Then go to bed. No other computer or streaming or TV or phone til you come back. Make an appointment in 2 weeks.'

Then I left to move on to the next patient.

He didn't show in 2 weeks. I phoned the emergency department. They were stupefied as they hadn't seen him in 2 weeks. They guessed he had moved with a sigh of relief in their voice. They at least had been told by others that he was alive.

Fiction starts here:

I heard he moved to Mongolia and kept a journal every day though I'm not sure as it was just a rumour. Maybe he'll put it on Kindle. It gave me the chance to take on someone on my long wait list. They too lived in the first world.

Hanging out with the Wasps

Suggested music – it would probably be something with a buzzing sound and who needs that as an ear worm?

Trigger Alert – those with Spheksophobia (fear of wasps) may want to stop reading or maybe this is just the ticket...

When I asked 'hey Siri', what use did wasps serve, she had a really hard time. All I could think of is trying to ruin camping and picnics.

I was camping once with a group, one of whom was quite scared of wasps. She would have to get up from the picnic table and kind of leave. This was very disconcerting to her as she loved camping and there were always plenty of wasps.

I randomly came up with an idea. It may have been fuelled by a combination of professional mind and cannabis.

I told her : "Stand up near the picnic table and stay still long enough that the wasps have lots of time to return. Now stick your arms out straight and out loud invite the wasps to land on you and sting you. Now stay still and wait to be bit."

Of course, no wasps went near her. She was fine the rest of the camping time.

The next weekend, she went camping with her mom whom I think is scared of absolutely nothing. She noticed that my friend was no longer scared of the useless wasps that joined them. She asked 'what happened? You don't seem to be afraid of the wasps'. I'm sure if her mom had been scared as well, she would have told her to stand up with her arms straight out and invite the wasps to sting her...

Flower Count - Victoria, BC

Suggested Music : San Francisco (be sure to wear some flowers in your hair) Scott McKenzie, live Monterey Pop Festival, 1967

Trigger Alert - those suffering from botanophobia, the extreme, unwarranted and often irrational fear of plants, should immediately stop reading and if actually in Victoria, leave.

One time I ended up in Victoria, BC. It was the end of February. In most of the rest of Canada, it can be cold and snowy. But in Victoria, the weather can be turning to spring. I found out that every year at that time, they had a phone number where you could count flowers on your property and phone it in. They then at the end of the week released some huge number in the billions of flowers. The whole point being so one could tell their relatives/friends in say Toronto while Toronto would be suffering a February cold snap/snowstorm. Total brag.

This year though the late winter had been unseasonably cold so the Flower Count folks were worried. I thought I'd help. I asked around and found the number to call at a horticultural centre. I had seen a freak dandelion that had already gone to seed. Was this a flower that could be counted? Well, these experts said yes it was flower gone to seed so was to be considered a flower. I immediately called the Flower Count to submit my count of one flower. Was it a flower or not? No, they thought not. 2 days later, I received a call that yes it was indeed a flower. I was so proud as this year the count would be about 43 billion and ONE. More numbers, more brag ...

Sleeping with sharks

Suggested Music : I was going to use the theme music from Jaws but it's WAY too scary and creepy ...

Trigger warning - those suffering from selachophobia (fear of sharks) should stop reading right now.

I left Puri, India right after xmas. The only sign of christmas had been some church bells as Puri somewhat oddly had a large church.

There were 1000s of kilometres for mostly deserted beach all the way to Madras. But it was a desert so very little fresh water. I was totally unprepared in the water category as canteens were not something currently for sale. But we started to walk by the ocean anyway. Very wide sand beaches and dunes.

First, we came across a large, beautiful but empty temple. It was in the middle of a very long deserted beach extension that created like a saltwater lake. The lake was full of fish jumping for insects. A huge number of fish.

It was very hot and I decided a dip in the ocean might help. I didn't realize the water immediately dropped off very steeply. A school of dolphins swam by me but they were definitely not interested in and were not giving free rides like in the documentaries. Suddenly I noticed one was different as it had a large fin sticking up. It was a shark following the dolphins in hope of scraps. I scrambled up that drop off very quickly as i wasn't about to catch the attention of any sharks. I never swam there again.

Then we found a few fishermen on the beach. They had dug a deep well where the water was only slightly salty. This saved us for a while. Then there was a very wide river with a tiny village on it. The villagers greeted us like celebrities. I guess they did not see foreigners very often if at all. They put us up in a wonderful temple and cooked us a fish dinner.

The next day, they led us to the river and motioned that we were to wait and wave down a fishing boat (dugout kind of) and the price across the river was 2 rupees (about 20 cents at the time). So the next fishing boat picked us up and knowing the price came in handy so we didn't get ripped off. It took hours to cross as the boat used a makeshift sail and the fishermen played a card game. Then they stopped at a tiny island that had red berries growing. These made a delicious sauce for their fish.

The town on the other side was much larger and had a train station. We realized we did not have any adequate way to carry water with a risk of few fishermen on the way. So we abandoned our walk. I often wish I could have had a large amount of fresh water and kept going. And avoided sharks and the jackal that liked following us...

Eating with the Newbie

Suggested Music : Relaxing Indian Flute *(*if you listen for too long, you will go to sleep but you can save the story...)
Trigger alert : those with aromaphobia, the fear of spices and spicy food, should stop reading right now. All my responsibility is abdicated...Then again, I think it is in all these stories.

Our first time in Delhi, we decided to stay in Old Delhi as it was way cheaper and you could take a horrible motorcycle kinda bus thing to New Delhi. I don't know whom but someone must have told us where to stay. It was alright for the price. The beds were fine, the toilet worked, the shower sometimes had hot water so it was alright, especially by Old Delhi standards. Though Old Delhi was something else. Extremely noisy on the street with all kinds of traffic. And the hotel was very tolerant so some of the guests were burned out morphine addicts (legal from the pharmacy at 10 cents a hit but still kills you, just more slowly). After a while, seeing addicts shoot up in the hall was just too much.
We did meet an American our age who had just flown from NYC. Now, first of all, that kinda thing is guaranteed pure shock as he had never been in India or a third world country before. Second, who the hell in the US had told him to stay his first night in that hotel...This was way before trip advisor and any guide certainly would not include this place (likely for fear of getting sued).

It got to be about dinner time, so we said we'd take him to our fav place. 'Do you like spicy food?' Oh yeah, he said he did. Now we really did like this place and it was super cheap. Maybe 10 cents for dinner with the rickshaw drivers. It had to be cheap as the drivers only made maybe 20 cents a day. There was nowhere to sit except on the street but then again, the whole place was on the side of a street. The drivers were the best squatters. The food was a chapati with a kinda lentil stew afloat with some kinda of wildly hot peppers. This was a mean trick we were pulling. The food was good and we were used to it but when our friend took his first bite, he immediately started to sob as it burned your mouth and everything else. A big cry. All the shock came pouring out. We calmed him down and over the next few days we tried to acclimatize him. I think we did. We had to split to the Taj Mahal and leave him behind. We told him to move to New Delhi.

I had travelled to Delhi with 3 other people, all the way from Istanbul. Within 2 weeks, the other 3 had left India as the culture shock was severe. They couldn't tolerate such things as the leper beggars, and I certainly didn't blame them. We sincerely hoped our new friend survived the shock. Maybe it was all easier after our mean trick and the fact that he had survived a stay in one of the most questionable abodes.

Eden Hashish Centre, Kathmandu

https://edenhash.com/

Disclaimer: cannabis is legal in Canada as long as you follow the new 26 laws which equate to basically making it more illegal than before. So the fact that this story revolves around a hashish store, it is only a story and not in any way meant to encourage the use of hashish or any other derivative of cannabis as it's illegal, eh...

Suggested Music : Katmandu by Cat Stevens (he misspelled it)

In 1973, Nixon and the US government decided that the hashish stores in Kathmandu, Nepal were a major source of hashish coming into America. Of course, this was not really true. At the time, hashish mostly came from Lebanon, Afghanistan and Chitral (Pakistan). However, the US decided that the Kathmandu stores should close. Rumours said that the King of Nepal and each store owner received a million dollars to close.

The most famous one was the Eden Hashish Centre, located on what was known as Freak Street. They were famous for their calendars and it was great as they were giving away the remaining calendars (now worth $200 for an original). Each calendar version had a slogan. My fav was 'We Serve all your Hashish Needs'.

I was there when they quote 'closed'. A truck came by to pick up all the hashish. We went through big barrels of hashish. Most was shit as the store sold mostly lousy smoke. I guess they did ship all the good stuff. But it was fun to look for soft, fresh pieces.

We immediately of course went to one of the western type restaurants to try it out ('no chillums allowed' said the sign).

The next day, the sign on the store said Eden Rug Centre and you could still see the outline of the word Hashish. We went in. There was now a beautiful carpet on the floor. The owner smiled and said 'would you like to buy some good hashish? And we just got some california sunshine (LSD) in ...'

Ridin the Rails, 1969

Suggested music - Box Car Willie - Six Days on the Road (goin to make it home tonight)
Trigger warning : suffering from siderodromophobia, the fear of trains, railroads or travelling on trains, should immediately stop reading...

Disclaimer hopping freights is illegal and dangerous...
I forgot that. Not recommended...Do not attempt...

The day after I finished high school, I was on the road. Hitchhiking to northern BC (over 4000 km) to harvest hay. Made enough to take ferry down to where I hitched to Vancouver. First time there. I was walking down to the ocean when I saw my first dumpster diver (I had a sheltered upbringing prior to my hobo days). Then just off the shore, was a large yacht with lots of partiers dancing on the deck - welcome to Vancouver...
So then I hitchhiked back - good rides til near Wawa. Anyone who has ever driven and certainly anyone who had ever hitchhiked across Canada knows Wawa. The place where you can wait days for a ride. Fuck that. We saw a freight train heading east and got on a top open rail car - bad decision as you get covered in soot and a sprinkle of rain tears at your face. Later we moved up to the extra engine. Train guys were good to us. Warned us where the train Dicks were, told us where food was

when we stopped. Now, the most important thing of course was not to be caught by train Dicks. Bad idea...

Don't get caught by train Dicks when ridin the rails. They must be cops that got fired and couldn't even make it as university campus narcs. And this is in 1969. Now they probably might beat the shit out of you.

But in 1969, this is what they did. Took you to jail (not nicely or anything as remember, they're assholes). Tell you that you need to spend the night in jail with the pervs or murderers or what have you. Then in the morning, bright and and early you see the Judge. The kind that's burned out from too many drunk driving charges and is prejudice against anyone who might be a hippie. He tells you that you have to watch this film then get the hell out of town and never come back. The film is of accidents involving people who hopped freights. Real gory. Missing legs and such leading up to the climax of leftover bodies on the tracks.

After that you get out of town as quickly as possible. If you're dumb, you look for the next freight. If you're smart, you hitchhike and pray for a quick ride. Even though you're still black with soot that the jail unfortunately did not let you wash off. Good luck with that ride.

ps - I warned you siderodromophobiacs...

Monkey Temple, Kathmandu, Nepal 1967

Suggested Music - Hey, Hey, We're the Monkeys - the Monkeys

Trigger Alert - those with Pithecophobia (fear of monkeys) should not proceed any further (and certainly don't watch above video)

Disclaimer: this story references illegal drugs such as hashish and LSD. Do not attempt. No responsibility assumed.

In the late sixties and early seventies, travellers, hippies, hobos and an occasional Saddhu, would ascend to the Monkey Temple in Kathmandu for every full moon (though in the monsoons it was only hardcores) and drop acid. (Disclaimer - do not do this).

It's a lot of steps up to the Temple so the idea was at the bottom, smoke a chillum and drop. By the time you got to the top, you were getting off. One caution. If you were to put anything down on your way up the stairs, it would be gone in a flash as the monkeys were thieves, cameras being their fav. Once, during the day, a brave soul ventured into the jungle along side the stairs. Brave as giant pythons were seen on occasion. He found a large pile of cameras. He said he only took the Nikons.

Meanwhile, as the sun set, the air was thick with chillum smoke. The rest was a trip until the sun rose, shining on burned out, stirring bodies, yawning or doing salutations to the sun. By the time you got back down the stairs, you could convince yourself that maybe a chillum at the Chai and Pie would rescue your mind. Always hopeful. The chillums helped with the acid hangover. I was told that some people just stayed at the top waiting for the moon to return. I was more the chai and pie type...

Land o Leeches

No suggested music as how could there be a great song about leeches.

Trigger alert : those with a fear of leeches or worms - this one is a big one as it has 3 names: helminthophobia, scoleciphobia or vermiphobia - should stop reading now.

When hiking in Nepal it is best to not go in the monsoons. There are some obvious reasons especially if you forgot your gortex at home. I got caught in the middle (3 weeks hiking in and then the monsoons hit which means 3 weeks out in the monsoons). One thing I found out is that not only are there those pesky leeches when you swim in some rivers/lakes, there are land leeches. You read that right. On the land, much bigger and they love the monsoons and tasty hikers. You go outside in the night to pee and suddenly you are encircled by land leeches, all moving towards you. It's the fastest you will ever go pee. Somehow they get into your socks and even though you are on the original salt trail, there isn't any salt around. Bad news. By the time I finished the trek, many of the leech marks were infected. Finding a doctor, lining up for hours and getting anti bs is another story.

There's no joke or witty ending here as how could there be. But there is a story.

This is the type of jungle that Baba Ji lives in. Baba Ji is a kind of ascended master who lives with his select followers but only comes out once every 12 years for the Kumbh Mela festivals on the Ganges. But it may be wise not to join the millions of other people there as every time there are quite a few people crushed to death by hoards trying to get to the Ganges. And somewhere in there is Baba Ji, not getting crushed.

But even if you do find him, it may not be wise to join him in the jungle as the land leeches there have got to be some terrible. I wonder if he stocks up on salt...

Told you not to read it.

Pleasant Afternoons in Kathmandu

Suggested music : *Katmandu* by Cat Stevens (yes, that's how he spelled it)
Trigger alert : those with cherophobia or fear of happiness, may want to stop reading. Also I would suggest getting professional help but there's no pressure...

I was told the Kathmandu Valley is one of the biggest valleys in the world. If it was square, one side would be almost 25 km long. The very best way to get around was by one speed bicycles. At the time, 2 people from the US embassy had 10 speed bicycles and that was a very big deal.
To explore much of the valley took many days. To rent a bicycle it was about 10 cents a day. So most days we would bike to a temple or world heritage site and just lounge. We would try to find a bhang lassi breakfast on the way and of course smoke chillums. These were perfect days.
Our favourite place was up a small hill quite away into the valley. From there, it looked directly into a famous Hindu temple courtyard. No one except born Hindus were allowed inside and that was rare. It seemed to be full of holy men doing various yoga and bowing ceremonies. We would nap there on the hill and just enjoy. The energy arising from the temple was very present. We always thought of the holy men as the real holy men vs many of the sadhus who were just into riding the trains in India for free (established custom that they never had to pay) and follow

hippies around for meals and hashish. Not that I blame them. In so many ways, they were true hobos.

We would look at a map and plan our next day's journey. Then head back to Freak Street for food. Pleasant afternoons. Except that one of the only restaurants with good food had a cassette player (good) but only one cassette (bad) of Carly Simon's *He's So Vain* which was certainly easy to get sick of.

Tatopani

No suggested music - your choice of relaxing music

Trigger Alert - those with aquaphobia should stop reading. Especially if you fear hot water.

Tatopani is in Nepal. It means' hot water'. About a 10 day trek in, 10 days out unless you do the loop which is about 6 weeks. Now if you plan it right, you can have 2 weeks leftover to stay in Tatopani for a week or 2. If you stayed longer than 6 weeks total, you'd get caught at checkpoints and immediately jailed and deported.

I see now it is well developed with numerous hotels. When I was there, there was probably only 7 trekking people on the trail so you knew them all. Now there are sometimes hundreds on the trail. The saying at the time was 'after 3 days walking, no bad people are going to bother'. There was one hotel when I was there with about 2 rooms. It also served simple meals depending on if there was a vegetable in season. There was an honour store front when you took what you wanted (including hashish), write it in the book and settle up upon departure.

There was only one hot spring and it was totally wild. The trick was that during the day it was way too hot (you could boil an egg which didn't exist there anyway). The only way to get in was to wait til about 1 hour before sunrise. Once the sun came up even for a minute, you had to get it out as it turned very hot, hot enough to burn your skin. And further bonuses were that it was beside a huge, roaring river that had carved out the deepest gorge in the world at about 24,000 feet deep. And right next to the hot spring was a waterfall coming off a glacier so cooling off was rapid. So it was chillum before and after. Every night at the springs waiting for the magic hour just before sunrise.

Part 2 : suggested music – anything by the Smashing Pumpkins...

So I was in Tatopani, every night at the hot springs, waiting for the water to cool. But when in Kathmandu, there was a tiny place called Chai and Pie as that was all they sold. The pies were fantastic though the route there down Pig Alley was a challenge. And yes they had pumpkin pie.

Now back to Tatopani. It was pumpkin season, so every dinner had a side of mashed pumpkin. We asked 'do you ever make pumpkin pie?' Blank stares from the owners. Well, they had flour, barley and rice so we thought surely some combination would make a crust. They had cooking oil. And because of chai, they had the spices needed to come close. So we experimented in the day and soaked in the hot springs at night. By the time we left after 2 weeks, the recipe was getting really close, quite good for desserts.

A couple of weeks later back on the trail to finish the 6 week hike, we met some German climbers who had come within 300 feet of ascending mountain Annapurna 1(about 8000 meters/26,000 feet) but were stopped by a 3 day blizzard. They asked if we had ever been to Tatopani as the hotel there had fantastic pumpkin pie, better than even the Chai and Pie. All we said was yes, we too loved it...I wonder if they still have it? I would love to find out as it is one of most wonderful places I have ever been.

Suggested music - The Polar Bear Song by Brandon Tobatto (not to be missed).

Trigger Alert - those afraid of bears (in the case of polar bears, this is wise if they are present), may want to stop reading now. There is no specific phobia name for fear of bears though zoophobia is fear of animals.

When we hiked across Baffin Island (Auyuittuq National Park) and before the complete route was closed by flooding damage caused by global warming, we took a boat into the 'wild' side. It's a 5 hour, freezing cold, expensive ride (hundreds of $s each) but we were fortunate to share with 2 other hikers. That side of the park had just opened for the season (generally only 2 weeks long due to ice blocking boats). You had to fly into a remote village to get the boat. The actual chances that a boat could make it through the ice flows were not great so you had to also book a flight to another access point and forfeit the ticket if you got a boat. The total flight cost was very high, enough to go to Europe twice.

You had to sign 2 papers before entering the park. The first said that if you needed a rescue (this was a very difficult hike with many rivers and glaciers to cross), the chances were about 50/50 as helicopters were prioritized to local medical emergencies and the minimum cost of a rescue was $10,000! Sign or no hike.

The other paper was one page description of how very

dangerous polar bears are and that the only way to protect yourself from being attacked was a rifle but rifles were banned in the park (so the risk of being killed by a polar bear were high). Sign or no hike. If you did see a polar bear and survived then you needed to go to the nearest emergency shelter (never more than one days walk away) and call in on the emergency radio. Then park rangers would fly in to look for the bear. I have no idea what they did if they saw it.

So we got to the trail head and our 2 friends had limited time (bad idea) and had to go ahead. The first day, a polar bear walks by them heading towards us. Fortunately, he also ignored us or didn't see us and we all survived. They radioed in the sighting and that part of the park was immediately closed. That year we were the only 4 to complete the hike.

We found out that a) polar bears are very big and b) we were very lucky. After we had left the second cabin, we later found out that a polar bear had broken the small windows after we were gone...as I said lucky. Wonderful 10 day hike, very hard, very lonely in a barren place of 24 hour light and danger...

Highly recommended (note the closure at Summit Lake and the deep river to wade across at the lake with large chunks of ice floating by). We took a year to plan the trip and always phone ahead as the hike is often closed, sometimes for years. It's called polypropylene or get hypothermia. Hikers have died crossing the river or from hypothermia. There are memorial stone piles for the dead. I never heard of anyone being killed by a polar bear. That is strictly up to the bear.

Sleeping with Scorpions

Suggested Music : *Send Me an Angel* by the Scorpions

Trigger Warning: Those with arachnophobia may want to stop reading.

We were in a part of the Kulu Valley in the mountains of India and just happened to arrive in a small town that was having a religious festival which is not at all uncommon. So there were no hotels left to sleep at. We heard there was a temple down by the river and we thought hey, we can sleep there. It was a beautiful if relatively wide open temple. Open walls, cement floor. The sound of the river rapids was soothing as I always find. There was one other person at the temple, a saddhu, setting up to sleep. He said nothing so we assumed he had some vow of silence. No one else was there which was surprising as with the full hotels and other saddhus, the temples are usually crowded with sleeping bodies. We had smoked a hash chillum and given that there is little to nothing to do in a temple in the dark, we all lay down for sleep. I was used to sleeping on cement as this was not the first temple I had slept in. Well, we found out why and why that saddhu was sleeping way in the corner. Well, scorpions, or at least these ones, are nocturnal. And the temple was in a direct path of their nightly march to where I'm not sure. So I was lying down in my sleeping bag with straight lines of hundreds of scorpions passing on both sides and I had little choice. I could not get up as I would step or land on them. I could not stay awake as I was very tired. Once I noted that they were always in very straight lines, I drifted off to sleep. I woke up to the sunrise and not a scorpion anywhere. It seemed they did not return marching the other way, at least not in the morning. Then again maybe I slept through their triumphant return. I was highly fortunate that I had not had a restless sleep. I found out later that they were not deadly but a sting would result in a 2 week strong discomfort. I didn't ask if multiple stings would result in what. And we were all alive, unstung and even the saddhu appeared happier.

Ghosts

Suggested Music : *She's Not There* by The Zombies (live on Hullabaloo,1965)

Those with phasmophobia, the fear of ghosts, should stop reading now.

I've had a few encounters. Once a plate came off the shelf and flew through the air for no apparent reason. There did seem to be a resident ghost in the house so maybe they were just pissed off for some ghostly reason. And if ghosts are basically spirits, then I know when I was holding my dog when she died, then there are spirits as I could sense her spirit leave.

But the strangest occurrence was when hiking in Baffin Island, holed up in an emergency cabin after getting soaked crossing a river with chunks of ice floating by. We could both hear voices of people walking by outside. We were too tired to explore and by the time we did, there was no one in sight despite being able to see for miles in both directions. Then we realized that because the park was closed right after we radioed in a polar bear sighting, there were only 4 of us in the park and the other 2 hikers we knew were miles ahead of us. It was very difficult by boat to get onto the trail so there couldn't be any late comers. We had no idea whom we had heard.

Later, at the end of the hike, a Park guide told us that a woman had drown there in a previous year. She had been trying to cross the river to get to the cabin. She had been swept away. We hadn't been...

If we had known about her, we would have complained less at the time of our own crossing about the river depth and our wet clothes and very cold skin.

Then at the end of the arduous 10 day trail over glaciers and many more rivers, the last cabin had a plaque : "Dedicated to ______ from ______ who died in this cabin of hypothermia in (the previous year on the same day)." I grew up in the same village. If I hadn't been exhausted, I may not have slept that night. Dedicated to the 2 hikers who had died fulfilling a dream.

The White Horse

Suggested music : Amish Paradise by Weird Al Yankovic

Trigger alert : Fortunately there is no firm phobia/fear of Amish except for trineophobia but that is not answered clearly by Dr. Google. However, equinophobia or hippophobia is fear of horses.

I lived in an Amish farmhouse. The rent was very cheap. It had electricity as it was illegal to tear it out which the Amish had tended to do in the past. But it had no running water and of course no toilet (basic outhouse included in rent). This was only a problem when I had women come over as the bedroom was unheated and some women did not like the post sex outhouse. But hey, did I mention the rent?

I was popular as I had a phone and all my Amish neighbours didn't. They were also often deaf due to inbreeding, so I had to make the calls. So I sometimes felt like SCTV's Farm Film Report. But I must say they were the quietest neighbours I ever had as my current neighbours are a huge pain in the ass. The Amish man right in the next farm had a spectacular white horse. Now I don't know if that counted as blasphemy but given that everything else was black, he did stand out. And he could hear and had the best maple syrup anywhere (occasion payment for phone rental).

I always saw it as an example of how it doesn't take much to be a rebel. Though it does seem to need to stand out and repercussions can be tricky. I know.

RCMP and the microwaves

(true story) - ycmtsu (you can't make this shit up)

Suggested video : Dudley Do-Right (Rocky and Bullwinkle)

Trigger Alert : If you have astynomiaphobia or policophobia (fear of police), you should stop reading now (maybe)

There is a village in Ontario, about 600 people, that in the 50's and early 60's was booming because of logging nearby and it had a train station. But then the station closed as the logs ran out. It became a ghost town with more than half the buildings, houses and farms empty. Then in about 1967, hippies (as it is not all that far from Toronto) showed up and bought up many of the farms. A 3 bedroom ok house on a hundred acres of rocky soil was $5000 or less. It also quickly became a centre for cannabis growing. One driveway that's 2 km long, at the 1 km point, a sign says 'past this point, it is highly recommended that you have your will up to date'. Right neighbourly but frowning on strangers.

Well, this general growing upset the RCMP (royal canadian mounted police). This was way before of course Canada supposedly legalized cannabis but in fact tried to put on a strangle hold of control. So every fall, the RCMP would bring in a helicopter and various officers to look for and bust you for growing cannabis outside. The local police station could have cared less about the growing so weren't much help at all. The village had one motel that not only did not welcome the RCMP but the RCMP thought it was too run down (they had that part right).

So the RCMP stayed at a nice resort on a nearby lake. Except, one of the first years of the police visitors, the resort discovered after the visitors left, that every microwave in the rooms was broken. From nuking weed to dry it quickly for obvious smoking purposes. They promptly banned them for life.

They never brought the helicopter back and were nowhere to be seen at harvest time. The local cannabis became known in Toronto by the village's name. 'Hey man, I got some _____ weed...'

Now with so called legalization, I don't think anything will change. People on the edge of town will keep growing more than 4 plants so they can sell to city folks. In the hills, large grows will remain. The local politicians themselves reportedly have grows there. The RCMP will still not show up and the local cops will still care less. The only dispensary around will still be on First Nation's land as it has been for a while as no one was going to fuck with them with a raid.

And the 50% Polish population will still get along with the 50% hippies (new and old), ever since the poison dog/vigilante incident. But that's another story. A good one. I hope it's in here somewhere as I forget. If not, maybe I'll add it or bow to popular demand.

Sleeping in the Khyber Pass (Part 1)

The Khyber Pass is a strategic pass between Afghanistan and Pakistan.

Note (for legal purposes) : This area is no longer safe in anyway so travel there is extremely dangerous and not recommended.

Recommended Music : any Reggae such as Toots and the Maytals

Recommended video : Making hash from cannabis leaves

Note (for legal purposes) : Hashish is currently illegal in Canada so this video is for entertainment value only. However, if you are aware of someone making hash, please send me an invite, I mean email...then I can keep it hidden of course waiting for legality before imbibing...

Apparently, there is now a train through the Khyber Pass though it may still be washed out. This would be quite the ride but remember the legal denial of responsibility above. However, before when I was trying to get through from the Afghani side, there was only a bus once a week. This was only weeks before the Russians invaded Afghanistan (yes, the Russians were the first to fuck the Afghans, setting the stage for everything after).

Sitting in a Kabul cafe, I discovered my female travelling partner had bought herself a ticket but the bus was now sold out. I decided not to play house with her anymore !!!

Now, at the time, Kabul was a nice place and all, even had a sad zoo, but a week, even with hash at a penny a gram, seemed too long. At the same cafe, an admittedly sketchy looking traveller, told me that hooking up with local transport would likely get me through to Pakistan. I ignored the word 'likely' and asked when the bus to Islamabad left (again...Islamabad is no longer a safe place).

The next day, I made it to Islamabad but it took so long that it was too late for the next bus. So I stayed in a hotel where I was very well treated (protected might have been a better word but I had a sheltered childhood so I took it as well treated). Now, though the bus to Islamabad was a nice mini bus ride, I was about to discover that the word 'bus' was subject to interpretation.

To be Continued :

Part 2 - *Do NOT sleep/stay in Landi Kotal*

(what the billboard sign said ...)

Trigger alert: For once there is none as a fear of bandits is apparently a good thing. But the thing was I had met much worse bandits...

As you may recall from Part 1, I was going through the Khyber Pass alone by local bus. The term 'bus' is relative as after the first minibus, the transportation changed to backs of large trucks with the goats and chickens.

After a myriad of villages and trucks, I arrived at the Afghan/Pakistan border, a place called Landi Kotal. If you look on the web, even Wikipedia has it listed as a 'tourist' stop. Even then and certainly now, this is a very bad and dangerous joke. One site even says the 'adventurous tourist' could tour the hashish factory and the next door factory that made AK47 replicas, solely with blacksmith fires.

The large billboard at the border said 'Do Not Stay Overnight in Landi Kotal'. Kind of a hint. Take it as real.

This whole area had a fancy name but it basically meant that there was no government and no police. It was run by bandits. Now maybe the name 'bandit' was a bit harsh. They didn't really seem to steal at random but had it institutionalized. Soon after the 'bus' left to go to Pakistan, the bandits had a roadblock. All everyone had to do was pay a toll of exactly what the bus company charged. The thing was of course, the bandits didn't have expenses such as gas and buses.

So these were rich bandits. When not on roadblock duty, they just hung out in outdoor cafes, armed with AK47 replicas, in part waiting for some Westerner dumb enough to take local buses. All they wanted to see was what happened when you took their offered toke off a huge hookah. Now these hookahs had a bunch of really bad tobacco as well as about 10 grams of hash. The entertainment value was when said Westerner coughed like never before as I staggered to the next cafe.

To be Continued :

Sleeping in the Khyber Pass (Part 3) :

How to roll a joint, Kyhber style...

Note : This area, including Landi Kotal, is no longer safe in anyway so travel there is extremely dangerous and not recommended.

Videos : use caution as some videos recommend a tourist visit here. This is extremely unwise and dangerous.

Now as I mentioned previously, the words 'local buses' is a lousy term. The rides got more difficult as the trip continued. Basically, when everyone got off a mini bus or back of truck with the goats and weird caged birds, I followed. This meant wandering through the village past cafes full of bandits, drinking tea and smoking hookahs (I wonder what they were discussing – maybe their latest model hand made AK47 which they all had). And as I referenced before, they were highly entertained by smoking up Westerners who coughed very hard after realizing that the hookah had large chunks of tobacco (uncured) and hashish.

I'd have to zip on down the street to catch the next truck to the next village to the next bandits. I would often be followed by an annoying man trying to sell me a piece of hash at likely exorbitant prices. Remember that 1 cent a gram was about the going price. I'd get to the truck and this time found it was a minibus, a true sign that Pakistan and end of bandits was nigh. This time, a young boy, I'd say about 15, shook his head at the annoying follower. And he showed how to roll a joint, Khyber style. The cigarettes there were poor at best, very dry, very loose and if lucky, few twigs. He with a flick of a wrist, emptied one into his palm. He took a piece of hash and with a couple of thumb strokes mixed the two. Now the trick. He perfectly poured his mixture back into the cigarette shell with about 2 pours from his palm, presto a perfect joint. Now this he smoked with me and we had an enjoyable ride that was otherwise bumpy, up and down hills and around precipitous corners. Often in Afghanistan, older Afghans would roll me huge joints but they only wanted to watch and laugh, not smoke. So I appreciated having a buddy to smoke with much as I appreciated arriving in Pakistan. By that time I had forgiven my female travelling partner for abandoning me, but she was no where in sight. No happy ending movie there.

An Evening with David Sedaris

Trigger alert : those with bibliophobia (phobia of books) may want to stop reading now. Then again, with this fear which also covers fear of reading, why are you reading this, unless you are in exposure therapy, in which case I'm Happy. There is no phobia of humour so laugh at will...
Suggested video : Santaland Diaries (there are various length versions) - the story read on NPR that made him famous.

David Sedaris, the author/storyteller, used to tour bookstores to read stories and sign books. The only condition being it had to be free. The first time he came to the local bookstore, he said there were 7 people. The second time he came, it was jam packed.
We were lined up to get a book signed but didn't know a future good friend was also in the line a ways back. The person I was with liked to ask people astrology type questions. As they already knew his sign, they asked him about his other signs (rising and moon). He said he wasn't really into astrology. I knew one of his agents as she is a good friend so I had a brief conversation. 'I know Kathie -----, one of your agents but I don't think she is your agent anymore' He said 'she isn't anymore? I didn't know'...
When our future friend got her turn, he immediately looked at her, told her her sun, rising sign and moon (all correct) and that she had a black cat (she did)...In his latest book, he talks about how

he makes up things in book signings and when he's right, it's great. When our friend read this, we all agreed it was just a lot to get correct for a guessing game...Did he write about fooling people and fooled readers at the same time? I wish he'd come back to the bookstore. Now he only seems to show at sold out theatres for prices I can't afford.

If you get a chance to read him, do so. Best to start at early books as many of the short stories are about his family so are somewhat progressive in time. He is hilarious, always perceptive. And maybe physic without having to advertise in the Farmer's Almanac...

Also, I would now ask a better question. Like 'when you go on tour, who picks up the garbage along the road that you do at your home' (He does that more hours than writing.)

***Author at the Pearly Gates** (a joke for a change)*

Suggested Music : Fade Away (Todd Rundgren live with the Metropole Orchestra in Amsterdam - recorded on iphones)
Trigger Alert: those with uranophobia, the fear of heaven or the sky, should stop reading this joke.

Now, I'll use Heaven and the pearly gates in this joke. However, substitute the Bardo/Nirvana/Swarga Loka/Jannah/Canaan if you want, though it may not work.
Fun fact (true) : Many years before his passing, Jerry Lewis suffered temporary death on the operating table. After he was revived, he was asked what it was like. He said, 'you know when you turned off the old TVs, it went to a bright light in the middle. That's what it was.' This is a precise description of the Bardo in the Tibetan Book of the Dead. Now the joke:
An author dies and goes to heaven. At the pearly gates, he is asked if he wants to see heaven or hell first. He says hell first, might as well get it over with. When he gets there, he is shown the special room for authors. They are all chained to a desk, waist deep in mud and their computers are running Windows95. So he says, no, this is horrible, let's look at heaven. When he gets there, he is shown the special room for authors. They are all chained to a desk, waist deep in mud and their computers are running Windows95.
He says 'But heaven and hell are exactly the same !!!'

And a booming voice comes from above:

'IN HEAVEN YOU GET PUBLISHED...'

Early Memories

Suggested Music : Sweeter Memories by Todd Rundgren

Trigger Alerts: Anyone with these phobias should stop reading right now and if the next cafe you are in uses chalk for a menu, leave...

1) Didaskaleinophobia – fear of school
2) Calxophobia – fear of chalk

I don't remember much before I was 11 as that is when my own pappy died. I only wish I could block out some adult memories (PTSD), besides my hobo days.

But I do for some reason remember a couple of things from very early school.

Kindergarten : Do I remember this or is it just from being told? Oh, I think I remember. First day of kindergarten and I was not impressed. I proceeded to cry as soon as I got there to such an extent that my Mother took me home. Bad mistake on my part. Next day my Father decides that if he goes to work a bit late, yes, he can take me. I think leave me was closer to the word. I don't remember crying as I probably didn't. I still didn't like it though. I began liking school just about in Grad school as they had a Grad club (read bar).

I wonder what grade? The teacher taught us first of all be careful with chalk on the board as it could make the worst screeching noise ever ! Remember?

And then one day she taught us how the word spelled 'island' was pronounced 'i...land' and not 'is...land' This I'm guessing was an intro to how English has silent letters...like k...nife.

Why do I remember that. I have no idea. But maybe that's why I live on an island and want to move to another island.

Now, what did your teacher teach you?

Now as a bonus. I don't know how old I was, but I must have been pretty young. My sister is 5 years older and apparently dropped me in the cinder driveway. Perhaps she was running. Perhaps she wasn't. No further comment allowed. But I do have the scare on my forehead to prove it. Thankfully it was small so was not to become a source of teasing in school. However, I seemed to have lots of other sources for teasing later on. Like when my ears grew faster than my head, and I've got a big head. So I was called 'Bullwickle', the moose from *Rocky and Bullwickle.* I didn't mind that – but rest assured the teasing and bullying got way worse...

4 days to Tehran – aka 'welcome to Tehran'

Suggested music : anything relaxing (such as **Erik Satie**)

Trigger alert : those with siderodromophobia, fear of trains, should stop reading right about now

In the early 70's, a catalogue came out called *The Whole Earth Catalogue* (1968-1972). In a strange way it was kinda dangerous. It definitely changed some people's lives and directions, including mine.

For me, it was a casual glance at the page that revealed a short description of how to go 'Overland to Kathmandu'. At this point, the only time I had heard of Kathmandu was a type of black hash. I had no idea that it was a place, the capital of the Kingdom of Nepal. While reading, I decided to go right there.

I'll skip the beginnings to finally get to Istanbul. The cheapest way to Tehran was the 4 day train ride - $4 one way with fake student card. With no food, no water, and especially no bar car. Everyone had lots of dried apricots and not much else. I find it odd but I don't remember any toilets on the train. I guess there must have been. I was travelling with a woman whom I had met. We arrived hours before the train was to leave. We didn't want to miss it as it only ran once a week. So we had time to kill near the train station. As far as we knew Istanbul was dry as in no alcohol due to the Muslim population. We were startled by a Tuborg beer sign in a bar window. No problem. 4 days of possible sheer hell ahead of us sounded like a good enough reason for a beer. We got us a beer each. Every time we were low in the bottles, 2 more would appear. After about 6 each, we realized that the train was indeed leaving soon. We had no idea how much these beers had cost. So as we got up to leave and began fumbling with money, the waiter shook his head and pointed to a man at the bar. Yes, he had bought all our beers...

So we wander into our train car completely bombed and face the why didn't you come get us comments from our fellow travellers. Our response of course was that then they wouldn't have been free – it didn't help.

So try being in a very cramped space with 5 other basically strangers and see what happens. Believe it or not, it took us about 2 or 3 days before murderous thoughts entered the scene. Especially when even the apricots were running low and we were forced to count them out or hide ours. Fortunately I sobered up so they no longer could bring up that jealousy.

Now the train didn't seem safe at all as at night people were constantly trying to get in our compartment. So we wedged it shut with a steel bar that seemed to be handy, as in used before. Overcoming my fear of anywhere outside the compartment, I wandered into another train car. I met a Japanese man whom I had met months before in Morocco. At the time, there were no Japanese travelling, especially young ones. Zero. He invited me to his compartment. Turns out he was now travelling with 5 Japanese women. He proceeded to pull out some Moroccan hash. Yes, all those borders. But then again who was going to search a Japanese. Come to think of it, I was never searched though I was clean. He lite a pipe and passed it around. Everyone smoked. The women just looked totally stoned. Now who would have thought they had turned it into a ritual. Pipe was empty and they all instantaneously, simultaneously pulled out an orange to eat.

I made it back to my compartment somehow. They all looked at me and immediately wanted to know where and how I had got stoned. After all, we were still in Turkey and I don't think the Japanese women would have been with me for 7 years in prison. So I told them how. They never forgave me. Me, I regretted not staying with the Japanese women. And really regretted not getting a small piece to take with me. I'm sure someone had a pin and a bic pen.

The rest of the trip seems like a blur. Not because of the hash. We were basically out of food. Everyone had told their life story in detail. I think we were all thinking that 'oh my god, I've never told anyone that...I wonder what they think of me now'. As a matter of fact, nothing. We were too tired, too hungry, too hot as we entered the desert. We all basically hated each other. We would have hated any 5 people there, no matter who they were. I once described Tehran as the shocking intro to the third world. Then I went to Pakistan. I used words like cacophony and claustrophobic. Like a smelly, dirty cloud suddenly descended. That was the train station in Tehran. There was a total crush of taxicab drivers rushing head long at anybody who was moving, standing or crushed. Yelling “Amir Kabir, Amir Kabir, Amir Kabir ...” (on the Magic Bus route – no longer exists). We were told that most young travellers stayed there. We stuck close together and did our very best to ignore all the drivers. We managed to make our way outside and wandered aimlessly away from the station. A taxi pulled up and we took it – yes 'Amir Kabir'. The driver seemed to immediately take us here and there, pointing out sight seeing spots. Iran was still controlled by the Shah and had the odd feeling of being in the U.S. Midwest. We were helpless and trying to actually appreciate the sights.

Eventually, we arrived at a sign that said 'Amir Kabir'. They could have added 'hippies welcomed'. So here were 6 of us trying to figure our how we were going to pay when none of us had any Iranian money as the train never stopped so how do you get money changed. We were standing there, on the sidewalk, packs all way bigger than we needed, blistering heat, dust and growing hate for Tehran and all trains, when the taxi driver leaned out and with a huge smile said 'welcome to Tehran' and drove away. No charge. Bodhisattvas can show up just when you need them. I often wonder what happened to him as it was not that long after that the Shah was kicked out. Bodhisattvas are protected somehow – are they not, yes?

You can beat city hall (once) - Part 1

Suggested music : Saving Grace by Todd Rundgren

Trigger alert : those with politicophobia (fear of politics and everything associated) may want to stop reading, though it almost sounds like a healthy phobia...

Where I live now there is no way to beat city hall as I have tried. They are lazy, corrupt and they take bribes (disclaimer as the proof would be difficult so take this as a nasty rumour and don't sue).

But in the city where I bought my first house, we beat city hall (once). The house was in an old section, a bit run down but up and coming. A drawback was the very run down 2 story apartment building across the street. We would make regular calls to Children's Aid as the adults tended to beat their children in their front yards. Once with a 2x4 !

One night, I woke up thinking I had slept in for work (something I never did in all my work years despite no alarm clock) as the sun was up. It didn't take long before I realized the infamous apartment was on fire, big time. Some people were jumping off the 2nd floor balconies. Now today if there was a fire next door or wherever close to my current house, there is one building where I would try to blow on the flames rather than call 911. But in this case, we phoned and even sheltered some of the families briefly until some agency found them a place to sleep. The place was really burned with most of the second floor and roof in bad shape. We were cheering in private as we figured it was toast. Not quite. The slum landlord claimed the insurance said it could be saved. Bummer.

Next - Part 2 - the second fire in the same building (there were 3 !!!) but don't worry, we win in a very nice way.

In Part 1, I described a fire that broke out in a very sketchy apartment building across the street. Sounds kinda dull but it wasn't and now it gets even better with the second fire. By the way, being awoken by a house fire is never dull. Shortly after the fire, the city had a local meeting about new parks as there were none in the area. We went to find out of course that there weren't any as due to lack of planning, there was no space left. So we very helpfully suggested the partly burned out building, even though we knew the insurance company had said it could be rebuilt (read cheaper than a tear down/pay out). The plus part was we submitted the only suggestion for the new park location. At least the city sounded sympathetic as in their nonverbal way, they were thinking 'gee. I'm glad we don't have to live across from that dump. It was bad before but now that smell...'

During the first fire, my friend who lived next to said dump, had the side of his van scorched. So he was well aware of everything. Especially after, yet another night of waking up to a fake sunrise as the partly burned building was now fully engulfed in flames. The whole thing. The roof was completely gone. I met my friend outside on the street and as he had moved his van, we discussed the pros of not phoning 911 as if a spark could just land on his roof (just a few little ones), he might be able to get a new roof from insurance. As we decided that the risk was too high, we also decided to go inside my place which was safe and to call 911 while getting a few beers. This was way pre cell phones but fortunately or unfortunately, the fire trucks showed up and basically practised with their hoses as the dump was total toast.

Two days later, stuck in the middle of the huge pile of burned shit, there appeared a sign 'for sale'. My friend and I quickly put together a plan to buy it cheap and sell it to the city as a future park (at a suitable profit of course). I blame it on our beer consumption as we were too late. The worst slum landlord in the city had bought it...

Next - Part 3 (stay tuned for the third fire)

In Part 1 and 2, I described a fire that broke out in a very sketchy apartment building across the street. Sounds kinda dull but it wasn't and now it gets even better with the third fire.

So now the decrepit house across the street had burned twice (second one was clearly arson). It was now totally a toasted goner. It was advertised for sale and was quickly snapped up by the person city hall regarded as the worst slum landlord. Somehow, it got out that he was planning to rebuild on the existing foundations (which were stone) but that said foundations did not meet current lot measurement bylaws by about 2 feet.

So one afternoon, it was hot, and I had my front door open. And I noticed that once again, even though just a pile of rubble, it was on fire again. I ran over to my friend's place across the street who lived next to the burned mess and told him to move his van which was now (again) next to the fire. Both previous fires had wrecked the side of his van.

He laughed when I called out to him. 'You're shitin me. Come in for a beer'. I guess the look on my face said it. He moved his van.

The fire truck showed, put it out, fire chief told owner to put up a fence and clean up the lot within a week.

We immediately drew up a petition(pre internet) asking the city to buy the lot as a park. We went to every house anywhere nearby and got 100% agreement. City bought it with glee given their hate for current owner and then turned it into a little park with swings and trees. A beautiful spot just in time for our daughter to want to use the swings.

I guess it was a win win as the city was very happy to get a park and beat the slum landlord. We won as it was a selling feature when we moved. So maybe you can only beat city hall when they are happy too. But it works for me. I've tried in both cities we subsequently moved to. Both didn't work. Like this story's title says: *You can beat city hall (once).* I'll be more optimistic and say 'hopefully once, maybe more if you are unbelievably lucky and the traffic and bylaw officers don't take bribes and/or are stupid' – which in my current city appears to be the case...

Bodhisattvas

Suggested music : Bodhisattva by Steely Dan

Trigger alert : though there is no phobia for bodhisattvas but because some might think as them as a kinda of angel, the fear of angels is angelophobia (true)

A Bodhisattva in Buddhism is the Sanskrit term for anyone who has generated Bodhicitta, a spontaneous wish and compassionate mind to attain Buddhahood for the benefit of all sentient beings. In other words, you basically have to make it though the Bardo and decide to return to earth to do the above. Sometimes Pappy gets into tight situations. Then I call on the Bodhisattvas 3 times for help. Now sometimes it works, sometimes it doesn't. I like to think it always does.

The one for sure Bodhisattva I have met was at the bottom of the temple steps of an Indian temple in a tiny village that I happened upon while hitchhiking (in India at the time it could be called walking as traffic was very sparse/non-existent). At the top of the long stairs up the temple, at a certain time, 2 eagles (very rare there) showed up for food from pilgrims. I knew this saddhu was a Bodhisattva right away just by looking at him. The Bodhisattva told me some words of wisdom. I often notice that these are the words most often forgotten. He asked me to tell him what it was like at the top. He had lived at the bottom of the temple for many years but had never gone up. Sure enough the eagles showed up, me with no food for them, and he was gone when I reached the bottom. He was nowhere in sight and given that this temple was surrounded by bleak desert, this also seemed remarkable. Thoughts such as 'did he really exist' as in on this plane of existence.

Once, I was staying alone in a very isolated cabin in the dead of a extreme winter. I had been very cold at night in my down bag but in the morning there was no way I could get that wood stove going. So I had to leave fast to try to stay warm, but my station wagon (my moving shelter) had a frozen battery. I had to start walking down the road even though I knew nearest neighbour was miles away. I was wondering if I was going to survive. This was a true, realistic thought as it was extremely cold. I called on the Bodhisattvas. Just then a hydro truck came along. The worker said 'I never come out here but happened to be nearby' (read killing time). He gave me a jump and I went looking for a new battery.

Now as I hinted, this calling on the Bodhisattvas didn't always work. I did it once during a very difficult and nasty work situation. And my lawyer showed up. Gave me very bad advice and I have suffered ever since. He is partly to blame for the symptoms of PTSD I have - him and the other fucking bastards. They were and are evil and I often wish they were dead and got really fucked in the Bardo. So it doesn't always work. But I have a feeling that if I ever was to find that temple again or be on that back road almost frozen, that the same Bodhisattvas would be there.

Kettle of Fish

Suggested music : anything by Phish

Trigger alert - those with the fear of intimacy phobia known by several names such as Aphenphosmphobia (which is the fear of being touched) as well as Philophobia (which is the fear of love) are cautioned about reading further. But honestly, that must be a difficult phobia and I hope therapy helps.

Full disclosure : I have never used this dating site Kettle of Fish or even looked at it. So don't sue me. However, I have changed details in this story so there is no way anyone can be identified. Though there is a crazy reality TV show where huge lottery winners look at fancy houses to buy. Like you really want people to know a) you won millions b) what you look like c) where you moved to...

I have stories of Kettle of Fish, told to me. The happy one, that's gotta feel like a lottery win, is last so hang in there.

1) Trolls - now they probably lurk on other dating sites. Women (and men) sometimes set up a number of identities. This is smart if it is 2 identities (though sites will block you if they see it) so that they can have contact with same man (or woman or variation) so they can see if he is consistent. Now, problems can arise as people get addicted to this and have lots and lots of identities and I guess get off on trolling. I guess trolling is addictive. 12 steps program suggestions for trollers would be interesting. Maybe I'll save that one for another story.

2) A woman who arranges to meet at a safe place, conveniently near her place. Once she gets a man there, she just wants cunnilingus. Not the sex trade. She just wants to get off, no money, no fellatio. And moves onto the next date. Playing with fire as some man might be over insistent about the no getting off himself part.

3) A friend separated from his wife after many years. But he definitely wanted to be in a relationship with a woman so he turned to the Kettle. He is very kind and gentle. What he found was interesting. His first 2 dates were I'd say very wary of dating sites (why they were on a date I don't know as they were clearly burned out). Their experiences with men were bad with them being abusive online and clearly trolling for sex. His third date was the 'silver tuna' a la *Home Alone*. They now happily live together for the last few years.

Told you to wait for it. Life is full of hope. It's addicting.

Stay safe.

Grumpy

Suggested video : Funny Grumpy Dog Pet Video Compilation 2016

Trigger Alerts : Those with fear of money (chrometophobia / chrematophobia) or with fear of piggy banks (no known name though some religions may experience this) or with cynophobia, fear of dogs, may want to stop reading.

Insert grumpy emoji (whatever it is – maybe just a dog).

Happy Pappy isn't really grumpy. I'm still happy. Grumpy is the name of my piggy bank.

I don't have many memories of my Dad as he died when I was 11 and I have only one thing that he gave me. This one is really important. At about age 8, my dad took me to a little store that was near the cottage. They had the most amazing collection of big piggy banks. Every kind of animal. I picked the dog. He tried to talk me out of it because it looks very grumpy. He's even got Grumpy written on the front of him. I was adamant, Grumpy it was.

Grumpy has become my most precious possession. He is on my dresser. When I was still youngish, I put pennies in him until he was almost full. At some point in my hobo days, I was flat broke and I mean flat because I was always just plain broke. Now Grumpy is a real piggy bank - no hole at the bottom. No way I was going to break him so I meticulously managed to get the pennies out one at a time.

I began to fill him again. I became fussy and only put in old pennies, especially ones with the king (I'm Canadian but old American pennies were acceptable). I also was forced to work at the Mint because I was on welfare (no fancy names at the time - just welfare). My job was on a conveyor belt looking for defective coins. This was very hard on the ears as stamping the coins was extremely noisy and they banned proper ear plugs. I am now partially deaf despite only staying long enough to save to get to India.

It was a very sad day when they stopped pennies in Canada. Grumpy was almost full. Lot of kings and defective coins such as pennies stamped as dimes and vice versa. Alright, full disclosure: I snuck a few out of the mint. Illegal but after all these years, please don't arrest me. Besides, I won't be able to hear you.

Now 2 out of 3 of my current neighbours are RCMP but what are the chances of them reading this...

Grumpy occupies the most prestigious spot on my dresser. Sometimes he wears a beret. He's still not full and may never be and he still is grumpy looking. I had thought of an electric eye that would woof every time I passed but no way my sleeping partner would appreciate that.

Good ride in the snow

Suggested Music : Sixteen Lanes of Highway by Murray Mclauchlan

Trigger Alert : those with chionophobia, fear of snow, or those with a bad hitchhiking experience may want to stop reading.

The 401 highway goes a long way, over 800 km and yes, it is 16 lanes of highway through Toronto. I only wanted to hitchhike part way, about a 6 hour drive if I had a car. It was early spring. The trick is always getting a ride through, way through Toronto as hitchhiking is illegal for most of that stretch. I got a ride past Toronto alright but it let me out at a really isolated exit. So I knew I needed to walk to the next exit to have any chance of a ride. But low and behold the police don't like that even though I wasn't hitchhiking. So the fine was just a bit more than the cost of a bus all the way. I decided to skip my explanation to the officer of how hobos have no money. I tell you he had no heart. He refused to drive me to the next exit so I could stand at the top of the on ramp part. He did however say that if I walked to it and another officer stopped me I'd probably get a second ticket. Like I said, all heart. I'm sure he beat up people as well so I didn't say much. I made it to the next exit no problem though it was getting unexpectedly cold.

By now I am way out in the country and it started to snow. I had some sort of warm clothes but it wouldn't be long til I was very cold. Standing at the on ramp with no traffic in sight, it turned out that a van had had to exit as well because of a flat. Now fixed and me turning white, they pick me up and were going precisely where I was going. Good ride in the snow. Hitchhiking karma is like that though it can go either way. Warm in the van or hypothermia in the snow.

Oh and I didn't pay the fine...oh I mean I did pay the fine (aka please don't come after me...).

It reminds me of an aside. One day years later, two police came to the door saying my girlfriend owed like a lot of money for outstanding parking tickets. When she came to the door, they wanted the money right then or they would take her to jail right then. She talked them into money by the next day which she did. (The tickets weren't hers – they were her ex's who would borrow her car, park anywhere and never tell her about parking tickets). As I was saying, officers (and exs), all heart...

Welfare

Suggested Music : Money (That's What I Want) by the Beatles (live...ish)
Trigger Alert : Those with fear of money (chrometophobia or chrematophobia) should stop reading and send me all your money so I can help relieve your fears.

Before fancy names, it was called welfare. Years ago, it wasn't so much that it was hard to get, it was and still is, not enough to survive. I had another valid fear. The office where I had to pick up a check, was just down the street from my Mom's house (I didn't want her to know) and close to my old school (my teachers might see me and they knew my Mom since she was their vice principal). So much for their math genius was what I could hear them saying.

When I went to apply for welfare, I got the stingiest, nastiest worker possible. I think it was because I lived downtown and even then their office was in skid row. He asked me what my rent was. I told him 50 dollars which was true as I shared a house with 4 others (yes, the whole house was 250 but at the time, this was the average cost of a house to rent as the area had yet to be yuppified). I didn't have a receipt and he didn't ask for one. If I had known he wouldn't ask for one I would have said $100! Then he added $2 for food. That's it. You read that right. $2 (two $) for a months food. So $52 total. I really, really should have lied about my rent. He said 'you can buy some rice with the $2'.

He actually said that. I can't make this shit up as even in fiction I'd see this as too cruel to imagine.

How did I survive? I have no idea. I don't remember. I probably had to drop home and 'borrow' from my Mom. I use the word borrow loosely as much of what I borrowed over the years I couldn't pay back. I didn't feel guilty though when she died and left us children equal shares. My siblings made sure that my major debts were deducted. Thanks...

Welfare eventually forced me to take a lousy job at the local Mint. It was so noisy stamping coins that I lost some hearing. But because welfare cases got the lowest jobs, I was on a conveyor belt line to pick out the defective coins. Like pennies stamped as dimes. So I would sneak a few out in my change. (Of course, I am just joking here as that was some kind of major crime and I would never do such a thing, though I understand they are now worth quite a bit...)

I did this horrible job until my common law split and I went hoboing in Asia. I didn't sell any defective coins as I could save given that even the Mint paid more than $2 a month for food. Besides I still had some leftover rice...

Fear of Parking Tickets

Suggested music : Ticket to Ride by the Beatles (Live at Wembley 1965)

Trigger alert : alas there is no specific phobia for this but fortunately it can be considered a specific social phobia in which case, I have no idea what to choose to suggest you do - read on or...

Oh, I got it. Here is a bonus link that may help : Wiki how to avoid a parking ticket - like really important ones, such as quote, 'don't drive, take the bus' and 'Read signs and notices carefully, and obey them'

Wow, that's like solved, right?

Here are two friends and why they might be afraid of parking tickets: (I know that I have referenced the first one before)

1) a friend went to the door one day (should of had fear of opening door) and 2 police officers - yes it's takes 2, said they owed like $300 in parking tickets from a city they used to live in. Turns out their ex used to borrow their car when they weren't there and park anywhere and ignore all tickets, and of course not tell them. Now this friend sold police on coming back the next day during banking hours (pre bank machines) and indeed they did pay the tickets. Personally, I thought hired thugs visiting ex might be in order (note that this is a joke as Happy Pappy is a dedicated pacifist though I have not experienced this particular

anti social behaviour). Although, hearing that the ex was beat up might have been very satisfying.

2) another friend. I think he just straight didn't pay parking tickets, probably broke. They too had the police make a special visit. However, they did not convince the police that they could get the money the next day and were still broke so were taken right to jail (do not collect $200). He phoned a woman that he knew had money and whom he wanted to date. She probably went for the whole package, if you know what I mean. (hint: fuck her).

"Hi, this is ____. I wanted to ask you out on a date but I'm in jail so can you..." She bailed him out. I'm not sure what happened after she drove him home but I did guess in above wording...

Moral of the story: take the bus like wiki says or at the very least, do not hang out with anti social people or act like one yourself...

My RCMP File

Suggested Music : Every Breath You Take (live) - The Police
Trigger Warning : those with astynomiaphobia (irrational fear of the police) may want to stop reading. Though it can be also fear of authority, so I don't want to tell you what to do...

In the early 70's, a friend worked sorting files for the RCMP (paper files, pre computer help). Of course, he wanted to look up his friends. This of course was not part of his job description and was probably illegal. He didn't tell me who else he found, but he found me. Maybe he found himself but then why was he hired? Either his sins were minor or the RCMP were making their usual mistakes. I thought the ones he found in my file were (right after scary), funny, and surprisingly incomplete for a hobo, I thought.
a) 'Received mail from Communist China, at age 13.'
My hobby was short wave radio. Not ham radio but listening to foreign countries radio broadcasts. Now, the fun was trying to find obscure countries, completely by chance depending on all kinds of things like weather and the fact that my Mom bought me the top of the line short wave radio. I would then write the station and if you were lucky, they would send me a postcard verifying the time. These were called QSLs. Some fascinating things - Swan Islands Radio was own by the CIA and sent out code for things like the Bay of Pigs Invasion. There were very sought after cards such as British pirate radio. The short wave dial was also littered with propaganda from Radio Moscow, Voice of America

and Radio Peking. These ones would all then send me more than postcards. Radio Peking constantly sent me lots of good stuff such as calendars and Chairman Mao's Little Red Book (should of kept that). Now the RCMP seemed to ignore all the other mail like Voice of America. The reasons seem obvious. But there you have it – listening to a Chinese station I guess at the time was a warning sign of a 'possible red', even at the age of 13. Hmmm... Good thing I didn't want to be Prime Minister...

b) 'Found in room where it was suspected that marijuana was present.'

Almost sounded like I was in a gang hit. No. I guess a friend had maybe something hidden in his room or at least the campus cops pounding on the barricaded door thought so. I of course had no idea that my friend maybe was a 'druggie' and nothing was found anyway. Campus cops were cops that didn't cut it as the real cops so being dumb was their biggest strength.

That was it for my file. I was hoping for more perhaps. I was fearful of more I guess. There was no 'Watches Mission Impossible every week'. No 'wanders country aimlessly' - though I think that might be on my current US border profile. I don't know. My friend's not there anymore so he can't check. I think he's wandering the country.

However, it is not very comforting that simply listening to radio or hanging out with friends, with never a hint of a charge, would guarantee an RCMP file. First part must have come from the Post Office, second part from campus cops. Good thing I never planned on being a politician. It used to matter though I guess it doesn't anymore. Now you can be the grand poohbah and a rapist.

Canoeing in the Snow – a true story (aka not a time to go cannuding)

Part 1 - the Call of the Water

Suggested Music : Going to the Country by Bruce Cockburn

Trigger Alert : Those with fear of water (aquaphobia) may water to stop reading. There is no specific phobia for canoes. Naviphobia is fear of boats in general.

Nope – not a good time to canoe. And actually this has nothing to do with cannuding (the practice of canoeing in the nude). I just thought it made the title sound more intriguing.

This is a true story told to me by a canoeing partner. It's about him, not me, and how he went on his first canoe trip ever – actually his first time being in a canoe or even seeing a real canoe – not just a picture. On the other hand, my first word apparently was 'boat' (I was 4 years old before I spoke, much to the worry of my parents.)

I must apologize as I can't even remember his name. Hey it was more than 30 years ago. Oh, Oh, Oh, I remember - it's Roland. But isn't that the way. Hard to remember this great friend's name but can't get names of my enemies out of my mind.

He is German. He told me that many Germans were basically obsessed with a few things. Alf, the TV show, canoeing (or dreams of) and going to Canada to go canoeing. So when he arrived in Canada, he immediately went and bought a used station wagon. It was October by that time and away he went canoeing. He had heard of this place called Algonquin Park and thought that was the perfect place to start/learn to canoe. It was almost Thanksgiving holiday (Canada). So better go before that weekend to beat the crowds.

He and a friend arrived in the park. He said there was even this place called Canoe Lake. Seemed like a perfect start in a perfect place. And the place rented canoes. The only thing was they were surprised there wasn't anyone else there. Such luck though the canoe rental man gave them a strange look. He didn't say anything, just a strange look. Canoe Lake isn't a huge lake so they quickly headed to the first portage. The 2 completely novice canoeists learned quickly as they had read lots of books and seen paddling on TV. He said he felt like a voyageur.

to be continued - Part 2, Lost

Canoeing in the Snow – a true story (aka not a time to go cannuding)

Part 2 – Lost

So here was a portage. They decided that checking the portage first was a good idea rather than carrying everything over. It wasn't a good idea as it turned out. No bears, that's good. Sudden cold and heavy snow, that's bad. Very suddenly they lost track of the portage that was very quickly covered in snow. Yup, they were lost in the bush with no gear at all as it was all back in the canoe. My friend was level headed at least and knew the direction that the lake was. So they bushwhacked through the dense forest. He said they got scared as they realized they could not retrace even their lost tracks as they were covered in snow. Later he laughed about not being able to leave a path of bread crumbs. But yes, they did find the lake but no canoe in sight. They followed the edge of the lake back through mushy swamp land followed by slippery rocks. They were exhausted when they got back to the canoe and their supplies. The fact that they had survived was really a feat. The other positive was that they had practised putting up their new tent. All they could do was get into the tent and collapse into their sleeping bags.

There can be a special feeling when one wakes up in a tent. Still cozy in your sleeping bag, you unzip the tent door to see the sun coming up. Very soon you won't need a sweater. There is a pile of leftover firewood from the night before so there is a deep sense of peace when your one match fire begins to boil your cowboy coffee.

In my friend's case, well let's just say this wasn't the case.

to be continued - Part 3 (conclusion) - a new way to canoe

Canoeing in the Snow – (aka not a time to go cannuding)

Part 3 – a new way to canoe

Waking up in the morning, the tent being heavy with snow was bad. The snow had stopped. That was good. It was much colder. That was bad. Their beloved Canoe Lake, where they had lost their canoe virginity, was frozen. Now that was very bad. The ice hadn't gotten totally thick, yet which was a life saver. They knew that beating the ice was going to be paramount. What would happen if they are in the middle of the lake and the ice gets too thick to paddle and too thin to walk. But this didn't happen. They had to break through the ice every part of the way. A new use of a paddle.

My friend said the rental man's look was even stranger when they got back. Maybe he thought they were goners. Maybe he would have eventually reported them lost (or frozen in the ice). They tried to get dry and drove to the nearest food.

One might think this would be the end of my friend's canoeing days. But all my friend did was sit out the winter and dream of his next canoe trip. He spent much of the spring, summer and fall canoeing. Not too early, not too late in the season as he never wanted to mix canoes and ice again. He quickly became an expert canoeist. By the time we went canoeing he had discovered this thing called white water.

His best story (besides the above Canoe Lake trip) was about the Finger Lakes in New York State and how there were small towns where Hurricane Hazel in 1954 had wiped out all the roads in so now the cars were all from 1954 and earlier. Kinda like Cuba but way closer. I'm sad we didn't get to do that trip. He eventually returned to Germany and I lost track of him. I think he's probably in Canada again either on the water or planning a trip. May the canoeing gods be with him.

'I can tell you how to quit'

Suggested Music : Take It Slow, Out in the Country by Lighthouse, Live at Carnegie Hall

Trigger Alert : Those suffering from metathesiophobia, the fear of change or changing things, may want to stop reading.

Milton Erickson (1901-1980), a psychiatrist from Phoenix, often called 'the father of short term therapy', used stories to put clients into a slight trance in order to encourage rapid change. Here is one of my favourites that I used many times as a counsellor (in between being a hobo).

A wealthy man comes to see Erickson. He tells him 'I am an alcoholic and have gone to many rehabs and therapists, but I can't stop drinking.'

Erickson : Ok, tell me about your life.

Client : I am very wealthy and own property all over. But my favourite place is a cabin in Colorado that is very isolated with the nearest anything many miles away. I go there when things get insane in my life.'

Erickson : Ok, I now know how you can stop drinking.

The client seemed in shock.

Client: How can you know so quickly as so many therapists have not?

Erickson : It's really quite simple. You get a trusted friend to drive you to the cabin in the warm season. Take 3 months of everything, food, everything but no alcohol, hidden or otherwise and no clothes. Clean out the cabin of any alcohol left behind in your cabin. Have your friend take all your clothes including what you are wearing and leave. You are now naked with no other clothes. Your friend picks you up in 3 months. You have stopped drinking.

The client stood up to leave.

Erickson : Are you going to do this? Go to the cabin as I stated?'

Client: Thank you Doctor. You have finally showed me that I don't want to stop drinking.

He never came back...

With thanks to Jay Haley (therapist/author) for writing a version of this story.

Busy at Work

Suggested music : Bang the Drum All Day by Todd Rundgren, live, with Flo and Eddie (the Turtles) on back up vocals

Trigger alert : Those with ergophobia, ergasiophobia or ponophobia (fear of work) may want to stop reading or may indeed feel validated if you too have been abused by overwork. You do something new well, congrats because they just added it to your job (with no extra compensation). But if you make a mistake or get too stressed, they'll fire you for a lame excuse. And don't count on the union – the lawyers are usually lazy fucks.

Some people think that government workers don't work hard. Maybe some don't. My friend does. Here is what they told me about an especially busy day. Note this is not about me - I suffer from the above phobias (all 3)...

“One day, I had agreed that 2 college students could come talk to me about working in the same profession as me, as they were considering (unwisely perhaps) to take it in college. I knew I had tons of emails to answer as my boss sent most of the emails at 10 pm at night but I was going to ignore that for now. It was the very beginning of the email curse as only managers and above had computers but they already were going nuts with it.

So after a few questions and answers with the students, the onslaught began. First, my pager began to go off (it was the time of transition to cell phones so I had both). I ignored it. At the same time, my office phone was ringing but I knew that could go to voice mail. Then my cell started to ring, and with no voice mail, it just kept going. As I went to get my cell off the desk, I noticed I had received 7 new emails during the brief time the students were there. I figured it was the same call so I began with a look at my pager, then answer cell but leave the office phone. It was 3 different people as it turned out. Just then, someone was knocking on his door. My staff never knocked on his door unless it was urgent as a closed door meant 'busy'.

The students were still there. Remember them? They hadn't finished but they thanked me, said 'I don't think we will be going into ______'. I didn't try to dissuade them - I had that no voice mail call (there were now 3) and I now had 8 new emails."

My friend now has an anxiety disorder and symptoms of PTSD...I wonder why...

5 days to the Post Office

Suggested Music : The Letter by the Box Tops (how not to pretend you're actually performing)
Trigger Alert : People are afraid of letters but there is no specific phobia. But if you have this undefined fear, maybe thinking up a name will help...or just stop reading further.

I've written about Tatopani, Nepal before. It means hot water so it has hot springs, undeveloped when I was staying there. I was the only one in the only hotel (read large house with one completely empty room). The hot springs were only usable at about 3 am as that was the time the springs cooled enough to get in. When the sun peaked out above what is the deepest gorge in the world, you had to get out really quickly so as to not burn. In the day, you could boil an egg assuming you could find one which you couldn't. So otherwise, I was bored though having unlimited hash at a penny a gram helped. There was a little store at the front. Strictly by honour. You would weigh a piece of hash and write it in the book. Coca cola was pricey as some porter had to carry it days to get it there. Anyway, when you leave, you add up the book and add it to the 30 cents a night accommodation (dinner included). I stayed 2 weeks and had to leave as my visa was running out.
I heard that it took 5 days to get a letter to the post office. Now I knew whom those men were on the trail, running really fast. They were runners to take mail to the post office, a 5 day run. Cool.

Like the porters who passed you going up hill on the trail, carrying 3 full packs (2 strapped to their backs and another strapped on top). Tatopani had no post cards but I had some tattered post cards left over from Kathmandu. Who to send them to? What to write?

Dear Eileen M.

I'm giving this to the runner to get to the PO. Sent on Oct 15, 1973. See how long it takes.

ps : Only pen in town is running out... Off to the hot spring to smoke a chillum...told you you should have come.

love, John

She said it took 3 months to arrive. But I didn't believe her since I was pissed off she didn't come to Kathmandu. This story was originally going to be published (with other ones) in a national mag but the editor left. So the chances of Eileen seeing this are a lot less (unless I send it to her) And what about when it's monsoons... And what do the runners do then? Trip? I hope not...those paths are steep.

The Dalai Lama and me

Suggested music : Inside the Taj Mahal by Paul Horn (very meditative by the amazing flutist)
Trigger alert : there is no phobia of meditation. How could there be. But if you have such a fear, give up and do what a Buddhist said : 'stop circling the cushion and just sit'.

I have seen the Dalai Lama twice. The second time was in Bodhgaya (where Buddha sat under the Bodhi tree). He was giving a rare talk to Tibetans. I had hitchhiked from Benares, all night on the top of a transport, sleeping from the opium most truck drivers insisted you eat. I never wanted to find out what they would do if I refused. They were kind and not nasty at all but they also always showed their hidden, very long knife (only frightening the first time I hitched a ride). Bodhgaya was crawling with Tibetans. I tried to get to stay in the sprawling mindfulness temple that was there. I was turned away as I guess it was obvious that I was not (yet) mindful. So I slept in one of the large tents set up for the Tibetans. When the Dalai Lama was speaking I didn't understand a word of course so I will skip that encounter. Also it was cold at night. Surprising cold. Especially when I was already earthing. Perhaps another good reason the Tibetans liked it in Bodhgaya in case the tree wasn't enough.
I remember years back he was giving a talk in Vancouver. They needed a stadium as he might as well have been a rock star. But the first time I saw him he was in Dharamshala/McLeod Ganj in

northern India. We were living for free in his old Palace (read cement empty rooms). I wasn't there all that long but spent my 23rd bday there. I think it was every Thursday afternoon he came out of his new palace to answer questions about Buddhism. There were a few Buddhist scholars there who studied at the Tibetan library. And us. About only 7 people. The Buddhist questions were usually complex. I was in awe as although he was yet to be popular, I had read *Seven Years In Tibet*. I never asked any questions. I really had no idea what to ask. I could have asked:

Me :'I want to spend the rest of my life meditating. How can I do that'

DL : 'Where do you want to do this'

Me : 'In Kyoto in a monastery'

DL : 'There is the road. Time to go there. Stop circling the cushion'

He had a way of answering questions but seemingly leaving the final part to the seeker. When asked what was happiness. The Dalai Lama said “kindness...”

Know what yr catchin

Suggested music: Hold On It's Comin by Country Joe and the Fish

Trigger warning : I have (among other things) chionophobia (fear of snow) so besides telling you if you have extreme chionophobia you should stop reading, I must admit this story was hard at the time and hard to write (but now Happy Pappy lives where there is rarely snow so please don't worry, I'll survive)

I was staying at my uninsulated cottage with just a fireplace for heat in the dead of winter in Ontario. Surviving that is another story about our 'good' friends Ontario Hydro/Hydro One. This story is about ice fishing that my fishing guide (the Fishin Musician) insisted on. I didn't have a successful track record with ice fishing but had not had many attempts.

We went to a local lake that due to it's lack of depth was good for white fish. I have no fear of fish so that helped. White fish are so good and don't absorb things like Ontario mercury. So we had an ice hut which was good as it had a wood stove that meant it was warmer than the cottage. Back then, Pappy still drank so I'm sure either 12 year old scotch or Jack Daniels was an imaginary help. As well as weed...tastes good in the freezing cold...

So besides keeping warm, ice fishing consists basically of smoking weed and staring though the hole in the ice hoping for the big one. I saw what I thought was a big fish cruise by and then return to be caught by me. Even my guide, the fishin musician thought it was a big white fish. We had no camera but a pic of me holding the fish and shivering on the ice would have gone into the cottage annals. By this time we were hungry and since we did have a lemon, we cooked that fish right on the ice. Fires look cool on thick ice.

When I came back in the summer (for the giant lake trout), my guide said “you know that white fish you caught? I found out that it was probably the biggest white fish ever caught on that lake. You coulda stuffed it and put it on the wall”.

So know what you're catching, record the sizes and take pics. Didn't really matter. We were hungry.

Hash Delivery Wala

Disclaimers :

1) under the current (de)legalization in Canada at the time of this writing, hash is illegal so this story is written in jest alone...do not smoke this at home...

2) Also, the Kulu Valley in India is no longer regarded as safe so travel safely and at your own risk.

Suggested Music - I Just Wanna Be Your Friend (Baby you know what I mean) - Lighthouse, live at Carnegie Hall 1972

Trigger alert : those with cannaphobia, please be kind to the movement and stop reading (or change!)

Kulu Valley, India, 1973

Every day after his school, our hash delivery Wala would hand rub us a tola (10 grams) of hash and deliver it at about a penny a gram. (Wala in Hindi means 'the one that has' and in hippieish means 'man' as in 'cool, man'). He couldn't rub more as he was very stoned from absorption by his hand pores. He was very handy as our house was about a 30 minute walk to town (but only 20 to the hot springs).

So if we were careful with the number of chillums we smoked, we would stockpile a little here and there. After we had an extra tola (10 grams) or so, we would make hash pancakes in the morning for 4. This was a true wake and bake. This was not a hot springs day but while we could still walk, we had an underground river coming out of the ground roaring beside the house. This was good for careful splashing as it was unclear where the river went once it reentered the earth.

By the afternoon, we would rest against the wall (the house had no furniture but rent was $3 total a month so we tended not to complain). We would say things like 'Can you move?' ...answer: 'No'... answer: 'Thank god' (shankar)...

The first one to be able to move well would make another chillum and hold it for non movers. And of course, wait for school to end so our hash delivery Wala friend could be greeted with a bow...and another rupee...

Fav/Unfav cities of the world – Part 1

Suggested music : Favourite song/video : I Saw the Light - Todd Rundgren, Daryl Hall - Live at Todd's House in Maui
Trigger alert : Those with cherophobia (fear of happiness) may want to stop reading and text their therapist.

Now, these are about cities of the world. Also, I unfortunately have not visited lots of cities in the world. If I'd been to Kyoto, it would make my fav list or perhaps I would have stayed there and not be writing this or have written it years ago in between zen practice.
First my favourite cities.
1) Amsterdam :
I've been there more than once and would go back there anytime. I do note though that it has become so popular with tourists that Holland is actually taking steps to discourage tourists from going there. In my 'deprived' childhood, I went to high school in Switzerland. So going to Germany or Italy for the weekend was standard. We couldn't exactly lunch in Paris except when we played hooky. Even in the 60's, Amsterdam had great macrobiotic restaurants.
My second visit was more relaxed on my own. I found out that certain identifiable people sold lousy hash that didn't get you anywhere. But the good stuff was fun. And the hostels were great, very laid back. So much so, that we never checked in so never paid but obviously came and went.

2) Kathmandu :

This one is hard to describe. Perhaps impossible to describe. I think you have to go yourself. Make sure your visa is up to date if you don't want a midnight deportation. Immigration police knock on doors in the middle of the night to check your visa. If it is expired, which is common given the difficulty getting extensions, they take you immediately to the next bus going to the border. There are ways to get back in but very difficult as your passport is stamped 'deported'.

This all reminds me of how I got one of my extensions. I had already used my 6 week extension to go trekking (they check that you have the stamp to show you completed the trek). But as you are allowed 2 trek visas, I went to get one. I knew I would be rejected as they always tried. I had no intention of going as the monsoons were too close. But as soon as I saw there was a curtain behind the desk, I went behind it. I figured either I would be kicked out or discover a wizard as in OZ. Sure enough, wizard time so I talked my way into 6 more weeks.

And a tip : Make sure you rent a bike and get around the valley. Spectacular.

A special note : I have no idea how they are coming recovering from the earthquake. I saw on TV temple Stupas I remembered falling down. I hope they recover well as it is a very special city and country.

3) NYC: Really, I do love it. I went there 1 or 2 times a year until I was 12. And I've been back as an adult. As a child I was

protected by being with my family, except for causing my life long fear of tall buildings courtesy of my Father taking me to Empire state building. I especially loved driving around Connecticut in my Uncle's 50's Thunderbird sports car, too young to drive.

When I returned as an adult, I could still find our family's old picnic spot in Central Park. I could envision my Father there. And then there is Strawberry Fields but I'll save that for another story.

Honourable mention : Varanasi (Benares), Barcelona (Dali Museum), Marrakesh (but not the rest of Morocco)

Next week : unfavourite cities of the world.

Fav/Unfav cities of the world - Part 2

Suggested music : Unfavourite song/video : I know you have one. Try not to think about it or mention it and definitely don't play it.

Trigger alert : those with enochlophobia, the fear of crowds of people and places that are known to be crowded places, may enjoy this story as it gives you 3 places to avoid.

I unfortunately have not visited lots of cities in the world. If I'd been to (afraid to name it), it would make my unfav list which is why I'm not there now and am writing this.

Here are my unfavourite cities :

1) Algiers

My hitched ride from Morocco to Tunisia will be a complete story coming up next. It's so bad that it gets it own story. Hint : 'Qu'attendez-vous? C'est Alger'

2) Istanbul

When I arrived everything was covered in black soot from coal fired boats in the harbour - everything. Now maybe it has improved but I'm not going to go to find out.

And when I was there long ago, there was a restaurant called the Pudding Shop, supposedly a hippie hang out (it wasn't). The wall was covered with a very large sign : 'One Puff, 7 years'. Nough said. Except for a description of the patrons: mostly evil looking men that you knew were evil Turkish police.

3) Calcutta

This is really not fair as I avoided it by hitching on a back road but this led me to almost sleeping with the tigers (see earlier story).

Dishonourable mention: Lost Vegas, Tangiers, Lahore.

'Qu'attendez-vous? C'est Alger' (What do you expect? This is Algiers) Part 1

Disclaimer: Contents of this story should never, ever be attempted. Stay safe at all times while travelling and know the various country laws.

Suggested music : Marrakesh Express by Crosby, Stills and Nash

Trigger alert : This could be considered an anti trigger alert as harpaxophobia, the fear of robbers, thieves or being robbed could be considered a healthy concern. But I'll leave it as a trigger alert because maybe your fear limits your life, in which case, therapy may be called for. There doesn't seem to be a phobia for therapy - go figure.

Well, it did start with trying to get the Marrakesh Express (which is not at all like the song). But just before going to the train station we stopped at our hotel neighbour to buy Goulimine beads (far out glass beads from a camel market in Morocco, seemingly no longer made, and wouldn't you know that I can't find mine), only to find out our van ride from Marrakesh to Tunisia had gone the way of a broken down van. So we found another van ride at the Fez campground. We get to the Algerian border and there's a long line up as they are literally tearing cars apart. Our driver speaks French to one of the guards. He takes our passports and then a minute later we see him waving at us from the front of the line. Gives us back our passports all stamped and opens the gate and waves goodbye. Phew...Bonjour...

Half hour into Algeria, our driver tells us he has 10 kilos of hash hidden in the van panels to smuggle to Germany...we swear at him as we all would have been totally fucked. Phew...Right after we give him shit, we ask how hard would it be to get just a little out to smoke...

to be continued...can it get much worse?...oh yeah...it does when we get to Algiers and you find out what 'Qu'attendez-vous? C'est Alger' (What do you expect? This is Algiers) really means...

'Qu'attendez-vous? C'est Alger' (What do you expect? This is Algiers) Part 2

Disclaimer: Contents of this story should never, ever be attempted. Stay safe at all times while travelling and know the various country laws.
Suggested music : Thieves Like U by New Order
Trigger alert : the fear of robbers, thieves or being robbed (harpaxophobia) could be considered a healthy concern.

In Part 1, we had hitched a van ride from Morocco to Tunisia. Made it across the border to Algeria only to be told by our driver that he had 10 kilos of hash destined for Germany hidden in the panels.
So we arrive in Algiers. It was the most crowded place I'd ever been (yet). It was filthy and incredibility unfriendly. We decided to go to the bank and get the hell out. We parked the van just around the corner from a bank and made a cardinal mistake - left it empty as we all needed the bank. Bank was closed so we were gone about 2 minutes. We were parked on a busy street with throngs of people around. The van had been broken into and the only thing they could get in that time was my pack. All I had left was the clothes on my back and thank god a money belt with everything important.
I threw up. There was a police officer nearby. When we told him about the 'voleurs', he shrugged and said:

"Qu'attendez-vous? C'est Alger" (What do you expect This is Algiers)

In a blur, we made it to Tunisia. The driver gave me a piece of hash and I knew my only hope was to get to Athens so I could buy some used gear like a sleeping bag and pack. Why didn't I turn around? Robbed in Spain at gun point of all my money and now this. I already slept with a knife. I can only say that Kathmandu was a very strong draw for me. Also, I didn't think that hobos looked back. Listening to Dylan in 1962 had stuck. I actually still had my American Express Athens market on the stairs sleeping bag when I left India. My Athens pack was long gone (stolen in India...)

One Psychic can Ruin your Whole Day

Suggested video : Last Week Tonight with John Oliver - Psychics. (may be hard to find)

Now if you believe in psychics or not, this is a funny if poignant video especially at minute 18 as he does a video of his pretend daytime show 'Wakey Wakey'.

And btw, the website he refers to is real 'mediumimpressive.com' (keep clicking for more free, fake readings).

Trigger alert : there is no phobia listed for fear of psychics or the supernatural (only of ghosts) but maybe there is a fear of John Oliver (televisiophobia is the fear of watching television, considered a branch of mediaphobia). However, watching John Oliver should be considered healthy.

When I crossed the Indian border from Pakistan (then and now an unfriendly border with a long no person's land that must be walked), the Indian border side had a woman beautifully dressed in a sari looking down from a perch above.

She is a psychic. Suddenly she may point to someone and say 'rupees in her purse' or some such thing. Bringing in rupees is illegal as they can be bought in Switzerland for way cheaper. They are also looking for hash brought in from Afghanistan or Chitral. Now if you want to know if she still exists, maybe ask a psychic.

I saw a woman get caught with rupees while I was there. It ruined her day. A friend at another time, brought in a kilo of Afghani ‘pollen’ (which can be made into hash with a couple of drops of water). He got through and was carrying a 100 Swiss franc bill in case baksheesh was needed if caught. Now it didn't ruin his day and was completely foolish (do not do this!). Besides he could have gone to the mountains of India and done just as well (also unwise). Also, the psychic might only take US dollars for baksheesh. All joking aside, the psychic staring down can really freak you out.

Disclaimer: Do not smuggle anything across any border. I met a person in Iran who came as often as possible as their friend was serving a very long sentence for trying to smuggle Afghani hash across the Iran border. That did **NOT** make their day.

Past, Present and Future

Trigger alert : If you have any or all of the following phobias, you may want to stop reading (especially so if you have all of them !)
1) past - atychiphobia (fear of failure likely based on past failures)
2) present - chronophobia (fear of the passage of time) is the closest fear to match fear of present
3) future - chronophobia - same as fear of present - go figure, go get therapy
Now for a further breakdown:

Past:
Suggested video : Mr. Peabody and Sherman original episodes (24) - pick one
Now wouldn't most (all?) of us want a Way Back Machine in our house. Maybe in the kitchen so it's really handy. Maybe with an app for that, in case you are stuck somewhere.
The biggest problem is figuring out what to change. There are so many things. That mark in grade 12...You'd need to make a long list which would cause the Way Back Machine to malfunction, increasing the likelihood of needing a way back. Be mindful of the past. Or is it be unmindful of the past.

Present :
Suggested music : Reelin' in the Years by Steely Dan
This one is SO easy to stay in the present. Google yoga and see how many types there are. Google meditation and see how

many paths there are. So the only question is why are you sitting here, reading this tripe when you could be 'sitting on a Zen cushion' in Kyoto...

Future :

Suggested music / video : guess what it is, using the below mentioned suggestions...

Take the past and present, heat in a beaker, shake well and pour. Presto : the future.

Oh if it was so easy. Well apparently it is. Here are some ways to predict the future. Pick one and google it. I take no responsibility for the results.

Psychics, I Ching, Tarot, Astrology, Sabian Symbols, Biorhythms, Farmer's Almanac ...

Did I miss any? It said I would...

Got a Pole?

Suggested music – (Bonus - Your Choice) : *Light Up My Room* by Bare Naked Ladies, *Undercurrent* by Tower of Power or *Power of Love* by Huey Lewis and the News (live)

Trigger alert : If you suffer from electrophobia (the fear of electricity) you should stop reading now, though given that where you got this to read, likely uses electricity, you may want to celebrate a perhaps small victory over fear...

As with most hydro, the hydro comes in on a series of poles, one placed on the border of our property and the next cottage. It leans a bit in the sandy soil and shows serious signs of wear (wooden). The cottage didn't come with hydro, so I believe this pole was put in by hydro more that 50 years ago. I get the hydro bills since I own it now. One winter, I decided to call Hydro and ask why every winter I would get a $100 + bill when no one was there and the hydro was shut off. Here is the conversation. HR will represent Hydro Rep. and Me will represent me.

Me: Yes, I'm calling to inquire about a hydro bill I just received. It is for $100 and I find that confusing as it is a summer cottage and the hydro is always off from Thanksgiving to about May 24th.

HR: Do you have a pole?

Me: Yes, that's how the hydro comes in. I assume without a pole, there would be no hydro.

HR: Well, that's it. You have a pole, you get a bill.

Me: So in other words, I can call this a rental for the pole?

HR: You can call it anything you want, but if you got a pole, you get a bill.

We exchanged other 'pleasantries' before the end of the brief, yet ‘enlightening’ conversation. It is just a cash cow or in this case a cash pole. I realized that the neighbours probably shared the same pole. So Hydro was double dipping the pole. Thirty years later, we still have the same pole, and I still pay rent. It's leaning a bit more now turning 80 years (estimated total rental cost so far= $30,000)

Someday (I hope when I am not there), the wind will blow it over and we'll get a new pole. I can only hope the 'pole rental' does not increase and I’m not there at the time the pole falls…

16 Foot Plants - Kulu Valley, India

Suggested music :You Can Get It If You Really Want by Jimmy Cliff

Trigger warning : Those with cannaphobia (fear of cannabis) should stop reading now – or try some and change

Disclaimer : do not try this as it may be illegal now and as mentioned in another story, the Kulu Valley, India may no longer be a safe place. There are a number of travellers who have gone missing here. Travel safe.

When we weren't sitting outside smoking chillums, listening to the roaring river in our backyard, we would wander the vast Kulu valley. We rented the house for $3 a month (yes, a month) so for the 3 of us, a dollar a month was not hard to take.

The nearest village was about 30 minute walk on river rocks, avoiding stubbing our toes as we had been earthing barefoot for months. In reality, we all had at least one big toe that was constantly stubbed and injured. A friend hiked up the mountain pass road and went to a temple to sleep. The monks immediately gave him a pair of sandals. My toe wished I'd been there.

One day wandering the valley, we came across a tiny village of maybe 10 houses. I don't think they had seen a Westerner for a very long time. And as with all of them, the front yards were solid hemp plants since they used hemp for many things. But given the amount of wild cannabis growing in the valley, some plants were basically female cannabis with huge October flowers. We motioned to the woman in the yard if we could hand rub the flowers. She nodded yes as this was not going to hurt the hemp use. But as the plants were 16 feet tall, one of us would bend the plant (tree?) down for the other to rub. We would switch off as once our hands were black, the pore absorption was getting us really high. We would wander in the valley and rub most days but this really would slow our motivation. As soon as our hands were black enough, it was chillum time !!!

And sure enough, soon two villagers showed up with chunks of hash they had made themselves. Everyone has scales. We paid about 2 cents a gram and left very happy...Villagers happy too...and even our toes hurt less.

Snitch (I would have used their real name but I forget what it was)

Suggested Music : My Old School by Steely Dan

Trigger Alert : Such a common fear but no defined phobia. However, being afraid of snitches is wise...

Disclaimer : This story deals with the still illegal activities such as possession of hashish, you are cautioned not to do this, and especially don't be a snitch.

This story came from an anonymous friend. It's false I'm sure...I have to say that to cover myself from lawsuits...

"When I was in university years ago, I would spend time upstairs in residence smoking hash with P. It was that hand rolled, round hash with the white mould streaks that urban legend said was opium. I know it is mould as I travelled where it was made. Now of course we know that smoking mould is bad for you but fortunately we are still alive and that kind of hash was really hard to find. Then after, I would play bridge all night. The person across the hall from me knew the score and I even smoked them up one time. Oh heck, forget it. It was a coed place and I was fucking her so she knew where I hid my pipe and stash.

Things changed one middle of the night when campus cops busted P's room. Now campus cops were cops that didn't make the grade as a real cop so that gives you a drift of how horrible they were.

So there was a trial and such. They were sheltering a teenage girl who was being abused by her father. Campus cops called that statutory rape against P. and his roommate which of course was a lie. Cops returned the girl to real abuse.

I always hid my stash in the communal washroom under the sink on a hidden ledge. After the raid, I discovered that my stash was gone. P. and I tried to figure out who was the snitch. He pegged the person on his floor who was like the floor leader and a jerk. But wait, my stash was gone so the cops knew more than just where P.'s room was. How? That's it, my friend across the hall was the only one who knew of my hiding place (and knew about P.). They were the snitch. I only wish I could remember their real name so I could curse them by name.

____ !!! That's it. I remember. (Deleted for legal reasons)...

Lousy snitch (slammer talk). They even wrote my Mom about it !!! Claiming concern when actually they were just angry at me. I can only hope they read this and think, oh my god, look how I ruined lives.

Fuckin lousy snitch bitch...and she was also a lousy fuck...

Timmy's Goes Hipster (aka London Fogs)

Suggested music : London Calling - the Clash

Trigger alert : Those with homichlophobia, the fear of fog, may want to stop reading since the word 'fog' appears here frequently. Or have tepidophobia (fear of having a badly made cup of tea).

London Fogs are rumoured to have been created in 1996 in Vancouver, so I'm a bit behind. My daughter told me to get one about a year ago and I'm hooked bad, thinking of starting a 12 step program for withdrawals. So soon after my discovery, I asked at Starsucks and I was told 'wow, we just started making that 3 days ago'. So I am in reality only 3 days behind Hipsterdom.

But every once in a while, something happens that shakes my faith. Such as when they started charging for air in your car/bicycle tires. I thought 'soon they will charge for the air we breathe' but then realized they already do (it's called a carbon tax). Then just last night, glancing at the TV ads during *Schitt$ Creek* (the amazing episode where they post links for people needing resources to help 'come out' from being gay/bi/trans etc. - Season 5, Eps. 11), I thought I saw an ad for Tim Hortons with London Fogs. I panicked. I must be hallucinating. I don't generally do that but maybe those flashbacks are returning. Though a few are quite pleasant if you get the drift. Then I thought, if true, I could write about this. I immediately switched to online and sighed great relief that no listing was on their website. Phew. Maybe I was just dreaming how awful that might be. Back to the Creek. Next ad...yup...Tim Hortons have London Fogs.

I was shaking in despair so much I had to wait to write this and rely on memories of shopping on Carnaby Street in 1967 as a way to relax...now, Step 1, 'we admit we are powerless over london fogs—that our lives have become unmanageable.' (apologies to Bill W.)...Step 2 ...

Now I'm off to go get a Fog somewhere else...a new way to wake and bake...right after the real way to wake and bake.

ps: don't get me started on 'impossible burgers'...

Miracles don't come with Warranties

- Full disclosure: title is quote from Schitt$ Creek by Moira (Catherine O'Hara) written by Daniel Levy

Suggested Music : Miracles - by Jefferson Starship

Trigger alert: Those with atychiphobia, fear of failure, may want to stop reading due to recurring thoughts OR read intently as therapy (we charge...)

I got what I wished for - sort of. For more than 20 years, I have asked the city to improve our street. Improvements such as a speed sign (existing single lane blind corner with current 50 km limit). Local traffic only sign. No stopping signs. Replace no parking signs knocked down on purpose (with full knowledge of police). No exit sign on cul-de-sac. Etc. I have written the city numerous times including pointing out that since I had now informed them they were now legally libel for any car accidents on the curve. Since then, I have been nearly hit twice and seen some very close calls. I must admit I relish if there was an accident, telling the people involved to sue the city and provide them with copies of the emails that would sink the stupid traffic people at city hall.

They did put in a local traffic only sign begrudgingly and on the wrong side of the street but nothing else. I also wanted the very large ancient house converted to apartments to cut down their chain tree as it seeds my garden. The seeds spread easily and the little fucks are hard to pull out.

So here's my sort of miracles. The apartment house sold and is being jacked up and moved forward for I don't know what reason except the property. Just yesterday, someone told me 'don't bother fixing anything in your house. They'll tear it down anyway (it is historic) – just sell it for the lot, you'll get 1.5 million...

...but the chain tree is gone. And the fire department ordered the city to ban all parking on the street as fire trucks could not get in. (Insert swear word towards city then insert OFF). For example, fuck off city.

So I wrote the Fire Department: (I usually only write good things to like underpaid techs in India). But I do write other things not so nice, like to the fucking cell phone company.

Dear Fire Department:

Thank you for ordering the city to install No Stopping signs on -------- St. The street is much safer now. The city continues to ignore other needed changes but at least the fire department has some wisdom. For more than 20 years, I had requested this and several other dangerous parts, such as the unmarked one lane blind corner which is city standard 50 km an hour.

If you do chance to speak to the city, you may want to remind them that bribes are illegal - not that anyone on this street has ever bribed the city. Heavens no...except for ...

But as you can see from my experiences:

Miracles don't come with Warranties...One tree gone, one tiny sign, a few less parked cars does not mean anyone slows around that corner. But I still have the emails so that city asshole can still be sued.

Cheese Cake Stories

Suggested Music : Gymnopedie by Eric Satie

Trigger alerts : People with turophobia (the fear of cheese) will be heartened to know that though real cheesecake is mentioned here, recipes and actual consumption of cheese is not. However, those who are tofu phobic, or have vegaphobia (fear of vegetarians/vegans) are also warned that the recipe has tofu and is vegan. As well, those with mageirocophobia, fear of cooking, please be aware that this story involves experimenting with recipes.

Now that the trigger alerts have taken up almost a third of the story, I almost had to skip Montreal and the cheese blintzes and get right into the recipe. But, I have been to Montreal on occasion specifically for cheesecake and cheese blintzes. Also, in the 70s it was a center for hashish. but of course I had no interest in illegal activities and only ate cheesecake and cheese blintzes. Another time, my hobo car broke down in Montreal and cost me plenty of dough and time. But I'll save that story.

Finally, the Recipe:

I wasn't eating eggs or dairy and had been a vegetarian for years, I thought I'd make a tofu pumpkin cheese cake. I'd never heard the word vegan but I guess it was. My roommates scoffed. 'You need eggs'. I used tofu, tahini, I think agar-agar too, canned pumpkin, spice and other things. Be flexible. You can make up your own measurements. Basically, kinda a thick mixture that bakes into something that can be sliced and goes with strawberries. The crust is another thing. It can be gluten free and very hipsterish if you can get some grounded quinoa in there.

My roommates ate it all with a request for 'more, Sir'. This time I thought - more 'organic' so decided to bake my own pumpkin from the garden. Big mistake. Too stringy made it way less popular. Last cheesecake I ever made. If the recipe doesn't work for you, don't criticize, just google it. The tofu blog.

The Air we use...

Suggested Music : Something in the Air by Thunderclap Newman
(for some reason, *Small Circle of Friends* by Phil Ochs jumped out - save it for a more depressing story, like this isn't depressing...)
Trigger Alert : those with mysophobia, fear of contamination and germs, may want to stop reading since this story refers to 'air' and you breathe air and - oh forget it, it's a stretch cause there's no phobia of 'air'...
(Note: written before covid)

It all started when I heard that air at a garage for your car or bike was to cost a dollar. WTF seemed like a appropriate response. So sure enough I get a flat in the driveway. And flat as well is that little, stupid tiny tire they give you to get to a garage assuming you are not in Death Valley (in which case you probably die before help/air arrives). So I make my way to the gas station. It's gone up to $1.50 for air. And of course, the little thing that pops out for a split second is rusted so there is no way to tell if the tire is still soft, just right (Goldilocks) or about to kill you in an explosion. And any hesitation may use up your airtime and cost another $1.50.
So I say to myself, pretty soon they will be charging for the air we breathe. Maybe some kind of yearly lung capacity test (mandatory) followed by your annual 'breath bill'. You might be

sent to some city like New Delhi were pollution means you can't breathe anyway. Or if you don't pay your breath bill, you can imagine what that would do to your Credit Karma score. How do they make money by giving you a free credit score. Or is it just a plot to sell the info to google, to sell to facebook who then sells it to the fucking russkies.

Then I realized they do charge for the air we breathe. In Canada, it's called a carbon tax coming soon to a bill near you. So we have come full circle. The oil company that charges me for air in my tire also creates the pollution that requires a carbon tax. Ok, ok. I'm guilty too because of my addiction to cars karma. So I should ride a bicycle but my tires need air and...you get the drift...

So you want to be employed...

Suggested Music - Who Can it be Now - by Men at Work

Trigger Alert : Those with ergophobia ,the fear of work, may want to stop reading as this story describes me wanting to work. And going nowhere.

I did want to work. Still do. So I write. I'd been screwed by a large employer, a manager and by the union. But that story I might tell on my death bed because they are such assholes, they'd probably try to sue.

I went to so many employment programs, I've lost track but I'll tell you the lowlights. One highlight. Note that each place redid my resume and did Myers-Briggs test. The top 3 jobs that came up in every test, I had already done.

First employment program. Don't know how I ended up here. Ended when on phone with counsellor who was at home and he had symptoms of heart attack. I called an ambulance.

Second one. Downtown. Big book at front with all half decent jobs gone if you phoned. Upstairs group was interesting but there were no jobs.

Third one. They gave out free bus tickets which I gave away til they cut me off. First counsellor said 'don't work at the place across the road that says 'help wanted' as it is horrible place.' Head counsellor said 'get job across the street. Your resume says 3 degrees including a Masters degree. Drop that. You'll never get a job with it. Come back if you want to drop it.

Otherwise, leave.' I left.

Fourth one : Very serious commitment to 6 weeks at college. Up grade skills. Teachers were great but I knew more math so all I did was teach math. Got badge for perfect attendance but no job.

Fifth one: I got extended pogie (employment insurance) to set up business. It was a long program but turned out to be a profit making scheme by a well known billionaire. But I did set up my business. Went bankrupt quickly as pogie ran out and only came across poor clients who couldn't pay.

Sixth one : this one required a disability. I think I used PTSD as that was close enough. It was a bit of a scam as they gave me new glasses. First they sent you to a psychologist who was really poor at their job. They gave me an insulting report. The actual program insisted that you finish a course before they would help you look for work. So I did a University upgrade in computers : got 8 A+s. And because I was now in university I got free counselling. But the so called ombudsman screwed me and I quit. The employment program got closed about the same time. Even screwed around their employees.

Others: one time I counted 11 programs I went to. Forget the rest as they weren't even worth talking about. I eventually gave up looking for work. Everyone of those employment programs is now closed. I guess maybe because there are lots of jobs.

Got one for me?

What's with the Lebanese hash?

Suggested Music : One Toke over the Line by Brewer and Shipley (live 1971)
Trigger Alert : Those with cannaphobia may want to stop reading as this story involves hashish which is currently illegal in Canada despite the so called 'legalization' of cannabis.
Disclaimer : see Trigger Alert (like do not do illegal things)
Disclaimer #2 : This story is not meant to devalue people of Lebanese origin. It is just based on true stories and Lebanon does have hash farmers. Please do not become offended.

In 1969, I could only get hash. You had to go to Montreal to have any chance of getting weed. And then only by the pound of Mexican. A friend I heard of would go to Montreal pretty regular by bus. They would meet 2 people who generally had just crossed the border and somehow had many pound bricks of Mexican weed. All compressed, there seemed to be no thought of female/male as it always had seeds. Good seeds that grew but had to be separated because they had a tendency to have minor explosions when smoked. Which were really distracting when this distant friend would either be stoned or getting stoned. There was also usually a fear of burning something like rugs or clothing (dead giveaways of use). Maybe a good price of $200 a pound, Mexican they told me and sell for $25 an ounce once they got the bus back. I envision it in a plastic bag in a pack in the bus – I have no idea why it didn't smell...

Now much more recently, that same distant friend told me they had a, prior to 'legalization', a Canadian Federal Government Cannabis License to Possess. Of course, when they flew to near their cottage, they went to a dispensary and they needed to show their Fed. License. Now this was illegal and the place was illegal but didn't get busted (then/yet). And low and behold, they see Lebanese hash in the display. F is for friend, D is for dispensary staff :

F : Wow. Someone does a really good job. That looks like real red Leb. hash.

D : It is. Just don't ask where we got it.

F: shit man ! ... I haven't seen that for maybe 30 years. It was all we could get unless you went to Montreal and got a pound of weed. And then on the bus back you had to worry about the smell of your pack.

So my friend went to the cottage and smoked it with a 'poor person's' Vap. A piece of hash, a clear plastic cup, a thumb tack and a bendy straw...All illegal due to hash. The dispensary now sadly lists as closed by the government. And Red Leb is just a dream again...

Update : the bendy straw is illegal as well cause made of plastic...

First Impressions

Suggested Music : People Get Ready (live) by Curtis Mayfield (the Impressions)
Trigger alert : Those with neophobia (the fear of anything new) may want to stop reading as this story deals with going into unknown cities, one with men on horses with AK47s (home made) and hashish...

Well I'm lousy with first impressions of people. I should have guessed the Germans in the black 'Mercenary Bents' in Spain were armed bandits. So I'll stick to 3 cities for first impressions : Vancouver (1969), Herat (1971), Kathmandu (1972)

Vancouver 1969 : Maybe because I had a sheltered childhood, I hitchhiked across Canada the day after high school ended. I'd never been anywhere much. My hobo days had begun. I got to Vancouver eventually and wandered towards the ocean. Isn't that the draw? I saw 2 things at once, both of them new. First, a man was climbing into a dumpster for reasons I didn't know. Second, just offshore, young people were dancing to loud rock and roll on the deck of a large yacht. I'd just watched a man land on the moon. I was incredulous (still am). Welcome to Vancouver. Hasn't changed much except gotten way more expensive – so more dumpsters, more yachts...

Herat 1971 : It's the first place in Afghanistan after crossing the insane Iranian border. The only transport from there was a hippie bus whose driver immediately passed out hash joints. First thing I saw in Herat was men on horse back with machine guns. Everywhere. No cars. No women. One hotel. One restaurant where there was only rice and a chunk of lamb. 'No meat' was about the only words in Afghani that I knew. Hotel clerk had hashish and opium. Hash was a penny a gram. (Don't use opium - it's not all Alice in Wonderland.) It was the poorest country I've ever been in. Made much of India look much better off and this was when India was still mostly poor. It wasn't hard to see where troubles in Afghanistan started. It wasn't that long after that the russians invaded.

Kathmandu 1972 : I got a ride on a truck from the Indian border, 2 day ride, 1 dollar, sheer precipice corners. Suddenly, from high above, I looked down from the truck to the vast, lush Kathmandu Valley below. Temples everywhere, monkeys, cheap hotels, restaurants with milkshakes. And the Eden Hashish Store. Their slogan : 'We Serve all your Hashish Needs'.

My Friend

Suggested Music : You've Got a Friend - Carole King and James Taylor live

Trigger Alert : Those with sociophobia (fear of people/friendship) may want to stop reading as Happy Pappy likes friends...

One time I did the MMPI (a long psychological yes/no test). There was a question I hesitated on. It goes something like : 'When you are driving alone in the car, do you ever feel like there is a friend beside you?' I knew right away that I had to tell a lie and say no. Otherwise, they may have said I was more psychotically screwed up than I am. Isn't that considered a sign of a delusion? Maybe... Besides, I really disliked the psychologist doing the testing. She wasn't professional at all and was clearly ripping off the employment agency that unfortunately paid for her services.

But in reality, it's a different story about 'is anyone in the car'. I often feel that someone is beside me when I am driving alone. And it is always the same person. Some kind of 'soul mate' whatever that means. I haven't seen her in about 40 years. I guess it goes to show that soul mates are not necessarily always together.

Then the last time I saw her she told me for the first time of her troubles (not to ever be revealed by me for sure). I don't know. Maybe that was the reason she never contacted me again.

Anyway, she still occasionally sits beside me in the car. I think about telling her different things, mostly just the scenery. But I still wouldn't admit that to the psychologist. And I wonder if I had answered the truth that 'yes' there is a friend beside me. Would the psych test have different results? My friend would still be there beside me, so the test was a meaningless waste of time.

My friend doesn't seem to be in my car as much anymore. Even when I'm driving alone along the ocean and I think how much she'd like the view of the mountains. I miss her. Psychological testing or not. Dedicated to my Friend

Note : I did finally find her online. I wrote and she did answer. She called me a 'flash from the past'. I didn't see that as an insult. She did ask if I lived in Kathmandu as I put that on facebook as why would I want trolls to know the truth. So I told her where I actually lived and wrote a short, friendly note. I never mentioned the seat beside me in the car. She never answered back. I realize now that the 'flash from past part' was an insult. She is certainly not a soul mate, and she is never in the car now. Cancel big time. I remember she didn't like the word 'fuck' when I used it as a swear word. So now I can tell her to fuck off in case she ever tried to sneak back into the car. I already feel I've met a new soul mate but I never found out exactly where she lives. So it's back to a coincidence if I find her again. She's not in the car but I don't know if that's good or bad. 'Suggested music' above,.substitute *'she (fuckin) hates me'* by Puddle of Mudd.

Dear High School (aka careful what you look up, careful what you see)

Suggested Music : My Old School by Steely Dan
Trigger alert : those with didaskaleinophobia (the fear of school) may want to stop reading as this is about high school and I didn't like it. It was also hard for me to write so my bitterness may show.

I didn't like high school. I've heard a few people say that they really liked high school. But their tone of voice indicated that either they were lying or they were surprised they did and were concerned this was not normal/common. There were bullies that harassed and threatened to that extent that I had to hide walking home and they vandalized things like shop projects and people's bikes. My Mother was a teacher and then vice principal there (read this was very awkward). I was depressed, though no one told me or did anything about it and I had no idea that depression was not just the way it had to be. I've always wanted to write to the current principal and say: (I think I'll send them this story).

Dear ______ High School,
There are many things I'd like to write but these 2 things I wanted to say the most:
1) I sincerely hope that you now handle bullies in a different way. Bullying should have a zero tolerance with automatic either long suspensions and preferably expulsion. I was bullied at your school many years ago and it affected my life. As a matter of

fact, when the high school had a big anniversary reunion fairly recently, one bully tracked me down online. All I could do was confront them to which they implied I had a mental problem. I know where I now live, things have not changed as my child was severely bullied in school. There was nothing done to the bullies (the school knew) and my child was actually held back though she is brilliant in things like English (tested as University level while in grade 10).

2) In my final grade, I had an algebra teacher (Mr. Kyle, whom I wish was still alive so I could send him a copy of this) who put a difficult question on the final. No one in an excelled math class got it right but he would not change anything. I have since showed it to graduate students in algebra who verified that the teacher had the wrong answer. I would have gotten 100% and I already had 100% in Calculus. So I would have won the top math prize but someone else is listed in the yearbook for the math prize. Please set the record straight. Signed, (withheld)

In the be careful what I see category, my search of a find your classmates site, I discovered that Alan, one of my friends, was marked 'deceased'. In the be careful what I look category, google listed 'breaking news' for the city : my high school 'was evacuated today due to a fire in the principal's office'. Do not worry as I now live thousands of miles away. I just saw it as very ironic. Maybe those old math class records self immolated...

I might have smiled (except about my deceased friend).

Note: written without prejudice so no lawsuits can be launched...

Strawberry Fields, Central Park *(pre covid times)*

Suggested Music - Strawberry Fields Forever by the Beatles (complete video)
Trigger Alert : Those with cherophobia, fear of happiness, may not want to go as it is a place of celebration.

I love New York. I really do. It started when I was very young. My Aunt and Uncle lived in this large house in the country and already had a rapid train to NYC. So I'd spend the day going to NYC. Just about every day I'd be there and I'd visit at least once or twice a year. Then when I was 11 my father died, we stopped visiting my Aunt. She was an amazing woman. Unfortunately, my other aunt was a psychopath who stole from us all.
Then awhile back when I was older, I flew into NYC and shared a ride with a high end, professional woman on her way to the Hilton. I got dropped off at what's called the White House which is a safe but very sketchy hostel near skid row. The exec was horrified and I was probably on the verge of an invite to her Hilton but I said 'if I'm going to write about hobos, better stay like one'.
I spent a lot of time in Central Park. The odd thing was that post 9/11, everyone was friendly and helpful. If I stopped to try to look at a map that has the streets so small you need a magnifying glass, 2 or 3 people would immediately stop to help me with directions.

I of course went to Central Park as I had done many times as a child. I even found the rock where I would picnic with my Dad. Now, in Central Park there is a place called Strawberry Fields, a 3 acre memorial to John Lennon. There are special gardens and quiet places but the stand out is a circle mosaic of inlaid stone with the word 'Imagine' in it. Every day, there was a man nicknamed the 'Mayor' who brought flowers and candles to surround the circle. His real name was Gary dos Santos and he did this every day for nineteen years. Sometimes Yoko would come visit. From there, as you look up at the top floor of the Dakoda where John and Yoko lived and Yoko still does, you can still see John Lennon's piano in the window. The ‘Mayor’ would take your camera and take your picture in the circle and you could give him money but only if you wanted. This is how he made his living for 19 years. Sadly, not all that long after I got my pic, he passed on. I don't think it would feel the same without him. It is a place of memory, hope and celebration. Strawberry Fields. Don't miss it. Any New Yorker will guide you ...just take out a map...

A Valley Girl's Version of Gestalt, Dude...*(best read out loud)*

I was editing this story I wrote pre virus time and thought it would be good under my Co(nona)vi(rus)d(isease) (20)19 topic as you could (like) do it at home. So here it is ... It actually does work. The valley girl stuff was drug induced.

The following was written right after a colonoscopy I had which included fentanyl and a benzoid injection from the hospital so i was looped but i still kinda like it – the story as well as the drug combo. It was based on a dream i had while still looped. Note: never ever do these drugs except in a Hospital.

Suggested Music : Rollin' With My Homies by Coolio (Clueless Soundtrack)
Trigger Alert : Those with oneirophobia, fear of dreams, should like totally do this, but those with fear of exams (no phobia name) may like want to stop reading, right ?

Like, you know, right? This is how to get rid of recurring dreams using like this hippie gestalt thing. ikr (google translation : i know right?). And like I know there's some hippie island off of Canada where some dude charges like big bucks for this, but like, you know why bother, right? Happy got me to write this for you, you know, like for free. And it really like totally works.

Like I got it to work for this like way scary dream about a big like stairway that ended in the air, like high up. So like let's try it on another scary one. Like school exams. btw, this gestalt trip best done in small group but hey, let's try it like solo, right? and like stoned is cool, you know, but it might like interrupt your dream memory. Whatever...

Let's totally do it. Just take all the nouns and like add 'part of myself'. Let's totally do it.

I'm running down a school hall part of myself. I like just remembered I have like a final exam part of myself and I'm totally seriously late part of myself. It wasn't on my sched part of myself. The class part of myself wasn't even a class part of myself I took, really part of myself? I can't find like the room part of myself and I got the room number part of myself, ok? But it's not like on this floor part of myself and totally need help (part of myself).

Ohmygod this is totally happening...

So like take your scariest, totally nightmare. It will like totally disappear. Really totally, ikr?

signed Totally Like Seriously Happy Girl (dancing in the room is like so totally good, right eh? For like Canadian girls too)... Right, eh?

108 Day Chant

Suggested Music : Ram Mantra Chanting - Sri Ram Jai Ram

Trigger Alert : Those with naviphobia or navisphobia (fear of boats) may want to stop reading.

I don't remember how we found the houseboat in Benares, India. We just wandered down the main alley until we came out to the end, and somehow found the landlord for the big boat. The boat had one large empty room with a 'bathroom' at the end. Bathroom in this case was a hole in the floor leading directly to the river. And the roof was a full deck upstairs. The rent was about $3 a month for 2 people. You read that right. Worked out to about $1.50 each a month so divided by about 30, you get the daily rent at five cents...

It was very close to a large speaker set up on the river. It was one of a series of speakers along the river ghats (cement stairs). The speakers were there to broadcast a chant of 'Sri Ram, Jai Jai Ram'. Think of this as Ram = a Hindu God, and Jai as a 'praise'.

We asked the owner of the houseboat.

'ummm...how long does this chant last?'.

Good question, right? (Did I mention how close and loud this speaker was, though they were all along the river).

Answer '108 days. You are so 'saubhaagyashaalee' (lucky), it just started. 'Shaayad' (maybe) you stay for whole time'.

At first we thought, 'They probably take breaks, and maybe it's like a campsite where quiet time is 10 pm'. Like they had a watch or maybe punched a clock and actual campsites. Otherwise, wouldn't it be really hard for us to sleep. And where was this chant coming from. Well if we had a watch, and were not smoking quite as many chillums and having bhang lassies for breakfast, we would have been more concerned about the fact that the chanting didn't stop. It turned out, it never stopped. They weren't kidding about the 108 day part. Non stop. 'Sri Ram, Jai, Jai Ram, Jai Jai Ram' .

We finally agreed we should go check out where the chanters were. Turned out it was about 7 men in a circle and clearly some of them were in a 'zone'. They just stared and chanted, looking like the exhaustion was completely hidden. We had to assume that the chanters were relieved every once in a while. The non zoneish ones liked us as we smoked them up and our hash was good. We chanted too and came back a few times during the 3 months we lived there. Didn't make the end of the chant. We just had to assume they would stop at some point on the 108th day. The sudden silence would have been somewhere between amazing and eerie...

108 Day Chant Part 2 (the Houseboat Deck)

Suggested Music : Happy Together by the Turtles (1967 live)

Trigger Alert : Those with potamophobia (the fear of rivers should stop reading)

I've written about this before. The deck on the top of a houseboat on the Ganges in Benares (Varanasi), India that rented for $3 a month. One of my favourite places. Why? I'm not sure beyond strange and wonderful things happened there.

Just a flat roof with a 180 view of the river. The river was moving slowly because it was not the monsoons. All along the river, tall temples, the tallest one with a line at the top marking the river level in a 1930's flood. The rest of the city would have been completely under water.

Things that pass you by on the river while you are either loading or smoking a chillum:

Flowers thrown in the river by worshippers. Two dolphins that had swam upstream thousands of kilometres to eat the sweets thrown in the river by worshippers. All manner of things float by including the bodies of holy men because holy men are not cremated but are given back to the river. Now admittedly this one is rough but rarely seen. And across the river, wide fortunately, hundreds of really large vultures waiting for the sweets missed by the dolphins and the holy men missed by nothing. Again, rough. You see the current there is circular so what floats by the houseboat going upstream eventually end up going downstream across the river, past the vultures.

A saddhu lived/slept up there on the deck, perhaps waiting to be floating by. Nothing else except us watching the river. But the sadhu decided I should have a rudraksha bead. They are seeds of a tree that naturally have centre holes and different numbers of symmetrical lines. Thus making a perfect bead. Different numbers of lines meaning different characteristics of people. He said 7 was my number of lines. He put it around my neck at dusk and suddenly a comet slowly flashed across half the sky and looking down I saw 7 swans swimming by. I never saw another swan there during my 3 months on the boat.

Maybe it was that. Maybe the stark contrast between spirituality and death... how does that make it one of my favourite places. If I only knew...

The GOOD things about Denial

Suggested Music : Say It Ain't So by Hall and Oates

Trigger Alert : those with alethephobia, fear of truth, may want to stop reading (fear of therapy does not have a name)

For interest sake only, denial as a 'ego defence' came from Anna Freud (daughter). Freud came up with the ego part. But since Freud was translated incorrectly, it really is an 'I defence'). 'id, ego, super ego' become 'it, I, above I'. (See Bruno Bettelheim, *Freud and Man's Soul*). Freud suddenly makes more sense.

More about denial. Here is a list of the actual many GOOD things about it:

1) it protects you as a child, as let's face it, everyone seems to come from a dysfunctional family, so parents must be very screwed up. So we need to be protected by childhood denial.

2) Denial is way better than lying. First, you don't know it's a lie. Second, it's guilt free. And third, even if you do know it's lying, you can later claim denial on the witness stand.

3) Denial also protects you from other icky feelings such as sadness, loneliness and a third that I'm currently in denial about. The only feeling that might arise is anger and you can easily deny that as in "I'M NOT ANGRY".

4) You just don't have to take any responsibility. Fault is not yours. (And you can always project that.)

5) Denial can help keep you in a negative state, a very positive thing for increasing your endorphins.

6) Denial helps keep obsessive thoughts strong so that compulsive behaviour stays in place which keeps depression at bay. Psychiatry says 'take away a compulsion and you're left with depression'.

7) Denial is an integral part of depression. Hmmm...skip that.

8) If you are a politician or a criminal lawyer, denial is like the mother lode of manna. (I have no idea what mother lode of manna means (beyond good) but it's alliteration at least…)

9) Denial keeps all kinds of therapists, psychologists, and psychiatrists in business and in many places, that has to be the #2 industry (after cannabis…)

10) and #10 was important but I forget, honest, I forget…

Tips for your Colonoscopy

Suggested Music : Laughing and Undun by the Guess Who (live)
Trigger Alert : Those with nosocomephobia (fear of hospitals) should stop reading right now.

Before I even get to my tips, read *The Happy Place* (in *Let's Explore Diabetes with Owls*) by David Sedaris. It is about his first colonoscopy and like all his work, is very funny. Trust me – you may need to remember the laughs.

Tips:

1) Have one. A colonoscopy I mean. At age 50 and every 10 years after that. Seriously. A friend, who is a great writer, died of colon cancer. He hadn't got one...

2) Rope in a ride to and from. You'll need one. Call them 'my ride' from then on. The bus after is no fun.

3) The sooner you see 2 days of preparation with pills and drinking horrible, foul liquid very quickly, as a cheap cleanse, the better !!!

4) Prepare a hick town joke to tell the Nurse. If they are from there, good luck. Here's the one I used. I live near the ocean so I picked a nearby hick town that just happened to be on the ocean.

"Did you hear about the tsunami that hit S_____ ? It did 2 million dollars in improvements..." I added "I hope you aren't from

S_____" She was but still laughed. Besides, I/you will be so high on the fentanyl/benzo IV, it won't matter.

5) Pick a hospital with a new wing, as this also means they have a new 2 million dollar tube with a great camera and the TV you can watch all the way to your appendix in HD.

6) Do NOT resent that the TV is way better than your TV at home. Doctors notice these things.

7) Be extra nice to your doctor. They hold the 'reins'. Do not tell them any hick town jokes in case they grew up there. Doctors notice these things.

8) Despite being drugged, do not tell jokes that make you laugh as any shaking of body is a very poor idea. I will let you guess possible reasons why.

9) Enjoy what is hopefully a rare every 10 year IV of fentanyl and a benzoid as it's a great ride. Do not try this at home.

10) Expect after when you are legally impaired for 24 hours to want to do something odd or obsessive. Once I insisted in going to a Thrift Store despite being in Thrift Stores Anonymous. Most recently I wanted a Dairy Queen milkshake despite being vegan.

11) Remember that person called 'my ride'. Well they better show as the nurse does not let you leave without personally meeting 'my ride'. And you are in no condition to walk or even find the bus/taxi stop.

12) Get a rare treat . Fill in whatever fav food you want. Leave out 'steak' – trust me...)

13) Enjoy and be thankful and overly grateful that 10 years is a long time. And if you make it to your #6 colonoscopy, congratulations, you made it to 100 years old.

Special Places

Suggested Music - anything by Eric Satie
Trigger Alert : Those with a fear of relaxation (a real fear) may want to stop reading. It actually does not have a phobia name.

There are times I take my memory back to what I call my special places. I do that when I can't sleep. It is a bit of a last resort though as I've probably already done other cognitive things that haven't quite worked for sleep. The other time is associated as I sometimes am depressed and suffer from obsessive thoughts when I can't sleep. I don't really have the compulsion that can come with obsession which is good and bad. I always say that if you are obsessive, you might as well have a useful compulsion. Mine was thrift stores but do to lack of funds and space, I joined Thrift Store Anonymous. I had collected silk ties and accumulated over 400. I really went for hand painted ones. My current problem is I can't seem to give them up. I gave away my Salvador Dali one (a good find) as the woman had a Dali tattoo. (This was a mistake to be so generous). But I'm hoping to get rid of them all before I die.

Now, remember this was about favourite places? My first choice is the end of the stone walk at the cottage. They are huge flat stones brought in in the 30's on the ice as there was no road at the time. I sit there and look out at the lake and imagine horses pulling a cart full of extremely heavy stones. Sadly, the stone walk was torn up in a recent rebuild. The large last one closest to the water remains for now but it's fate is unknown. I'll still use it as a memory.

Another favourite place is a place my daughter and I used to visit when she was young. It's a secret so I can't tell you. A third favourite place is the top deck of a house boat we rented in Benares (Varanasi), India. I've already written a little about this previously in case you missed it. The story is called '108 day chant' as that was what it was. But there was so much more when on the deck, watching the Ganges do it's thing. The slow movement in no monsoons weather brings wonders and occasional bleakness. Is that the right word? Bleak? As since holy men and babies are not cremated in this holy city, very rarely a body may float slowly by. I guess that might be more than 'bleak'. But what happens to the bodies after is way more than bleak so I'll skip that part of the memory. Still the deck is a special place when the dolphins that have swam upstream thousands of miles to get the holy food that's thrown into the river – well that seems special. So enjoy your fav places and maybe use these thoughts of yours to fall asleep. Or even better, go to your special places again, though I don't think I'll make it back to Benares...

My therapist recently taught me how to take my mind to being in a kayak, at 4 am when I can't sleep...(a positive obsessive thought...)

Fear of Squirrels (Revised)

Suggested Music : I Wanna Be Sedated by the Ramones
Trigger Alert : those with sciurophobia (fear of squirrels) should absolutely stop reading right now

Ok, ok. I always write stories with trigger alerts and phobias. Besides being afraid of heights (acrophobic), I'm afraid of squirrels or at least must be due to the recurring nightmares I have. Back to the heights, I thought I'd cure it by rock climbing with ropes and such, even go to 5.7 (difficulty level) which for me I thought was good, but ultimately did not cure it. I used to use the side visor when I drove by the CN Tower so I wouldn't feel really ill.

How's that for getting away from discussing squirrels. I think it started because one year a squirrel got into our attic and proceeded to have 2 pain in the ass babies. I had the hole fixed at least 3 times before finally having the section of house corner ripped out and new flashing wrapped around everywhere! Even then, one comes back to look at the same corner.

I'm now not afraid when I see them. I get excited because I have a spray gun with water and ammonia that goes 30 feet. They hate the smell and a good hit sometimes means no return.

But the nightmares. One story I wrote for here was about if a valley girl did a gestalt dream interpretation that often results in the recurring nightmare going bye bye. Let's do it here straight as in no valley girl lingo. The idea being to tell someone or a group the nightmare by following every noun by 'part of myself'. Some kind of personal, deep control of dreams.

I am in the bedroom part of myself, and its night part of myself and I'm off to my 4 am piss part of myself, and suddenly there is a squirrel part of myself in the hall part of myself running towards me part of myself to attack. I scream part of myself as I wake up .

There. I'll let you know if it works...now what about that cliff (part of myself) nightmare...

Addendum : 9 months later and no squirrel nightmares. It works. Also 2 things : I almost got a squirrel trap for xmas. My former neighbour did that and then drowned them. It might sound like very bad karma but it is legal here as they are invasive. Number 2 : to the student who brought 2 squirrels from Vancouver to Vancouver Island because she thought they were cute and let them go at her fancy private school...fuck off and I HATE you...

Path to a Pescetarian

Suggested Music : Lovin Spoonful (live on Hullabaloo, 1965) - You Didn't Have To Be So Nice (I Would Have Loved You Anyway)
Trigger Alert : Those with lachanophobia (fear of vegetables) or ichthyophobia (fear of fish) may not want to keep reading.

My path of almost 50 years, a carnivore, then vegetarian then macrobiotic then pescetarian (for the protein).
1) I had lived with vegetarians after university and then lived in India, so it just happened. I once told a man who was about 25 that I'd been vegetarian at that time for 20 years. I somehow used to say this with a false sense of pride. This may have been the last time any condescending pride escaped. He said 'my parents are vegetarian. I've never eaten meat in my life.' (No pride in voice). By the way, he was healthy, very energetic and talented. And I grew up refusing to eat things like squash...dumb/spoiled periods of life.
2) I was once in a Spanish jail (which I have previously written about as the cell was filled with women being charged for sex trade). I was not under arrest as I had been robbed at gun point and had nowhere to stay. The guards (Franco time) all had AK47 things but kindly arranged for a free meal. The restaurant of course gave me a big piece of meat. What could I do but eat it, thank them and have my tummy do the regret and return to my

newfound friendly jail mates...I had a pack of smokes the thieves missed. Last time I ate meat (1974).

3) Recently I went to my fav Jamaican patty joint. I always say 'vegetarian whatever' as the owner chooses well. He said the usual : 'How long you been a veg?' '46 years' 'Why?' 'It's so long I don't remember' (My standard answer.) He didn't buy it. But it's at least partly true...that and it's too late as my body would freak. My friend helped by saying ' he cheats. he eats fish'. I saved by saying I had caught 22 lake trout ... My patty walla lost interest. I think he dismissed me. But I'll still order 'veg whatever' next time.

4) so someone might think a 50 year no meat would be healthy ... right ?!? Actually not necessarily. My ulcers predate anything caused by being forced to drink milk as a child. But a stroke at age 56 doesn't fit the healthy schedule. I'll blame that on years of smoking Turkish tobacco which most likely is true.

Fishin (in memory of my friend and fishing guide, Carl)

Suggested Video : The Fishin' Musician - Hot Air Balloon Fishing, John Candy with JimmyBuffett
and Music Video : Jimmy Buffett on the Fishin' Musician
Trigger Alert : Those with ichthyophobia (fear of fish) may want to stop reading. Those with globophobia (fear of balloons) may not want to watch the above video.

I like to fish. Now admittedly, I don't like killing them. So I have a guide who handles everything. He's got the boat, down riggers, best hooks, the works. I call him the fishin musician like John Candy in the video. He of course never drinks alcohol or smokes weed while fishing (true) as that's illegal and of course I would never want to smoke a joint while patiently awaiting that big bite (untrue).

Two best times fishing:

Musky fishing and the trout fishing time we caught a lot. Now musky are amazing fish to catch though lousy to eat but a 6 footer looks really good on the wall. The musky comes up to get the bait and flips way up in the air. It can take many days of fishing just to get one in the boat. That day, we got 2 to the boat that got away, one in the boat that was almost 4 feet long. We threw it back as we had set 6 feet as the minimum keeper. One bite swallowed one whole long hook and then bit through the second long hook. That was the 6 footer that got away.

And then the time the fishin musician took me out but said it was too early in the spring so the lake had not 'turned', so we might not get any. We caught 22 lake trout that day. He had never caught that many. Most were keepers but we threw back all but 2 as that's what we needed for eating. Both about 15 pounds. Special lake trout stocked in that lake many years ago (and only that lake). The record there is 42 pounds !!!
Can't wait to go again this year. There is a hidden crater where you catch your limit of rainbow trout in minutes and party after that but it is across 2 lakes and a rough canoe portage in mosquito infested bush...but rainbow are such good eatin...Maybe this year... Enjoy...

Memorandum : My fishin musician got prostate cancer which spread to his bones. As I write this, he is dying and couldn't take me fishing. What am I to do ??? ...

Stroke

Suggested Music : These Eyes by the Guess Who (live)
Trigger Alert - Those with iatrophobia (fear of doctors) may want to stop reading.

I'm lucky. Now I have a family doctor which here is like winning a lottery. And he's great. He is constantly joking or laughing and yet somehow gets all points done. I go with a list of usually about 7 things and he always gets done on time. He is usually early as he says “my time is valuable, so is yours...” I won the said lottery as I had gone to a walk-in clinic like most people here as most people don't have a doctor. He said after seeing me if I wanted a regular doctor. I of course said yes but how was this possible? He said he worked in Emergency for years but got sick of people being there basically because they couldn't find a regular doctor. So he changed to a family doctor.
But I'm also unlucky. 15 years ago, I stood up and suddenly couldn't see out my right eye. I had no idea what was going on but ended up at Emergency. They triaged me right away but you never want to have to go to Emerg on a Sunday evening. They don't have enough doctors so they had an intern on who didn't know fuck. She did nothing except call the eye specialist on call. Oh and she said 'I have real emergencies to take care of'. The specialist took 5 hours to arrive as I guess he wasn't finished his golf game. He had some fancy equipment but told me very little

except that I had had stroke. Maybe he realized it was now too late. They sent me home. I had permanently lost that eye.

I later found out that there is an injection you can get called a TBA that will loosen clots (a clot was blocking my optic nerve until it died). But did the fucking doctor do this or mention it. NO. It is best to get the drug within 3 hours of the stroke to up to 4.5 hours. Was I in time? Yes...

Having one eye means I have no depth perception so parking and stairs are difficult at best. So I have a handicap thing for my car. I once parked at the local yuppie mall in one the special handicap parking spots. A man confronted me asking how I got a handicap sticker. I told him about the blind eye but he scoffed, thinking I shouldn't get one. I said 'If you want to complain, the mall manager's office is right there or call the police. When you want me, I'll be in the grocery store...Or even better I would suggest you go home first. Make an eye patch and drive back here and find parking. But remember, when you all are looking for me to arrest me for misuse of the parking spot, I'm in the store right there. He didn't say a word but disappeared quickly. POOOF !!!

What facebook Knows/Guesses About Me

Suggested Music : Outside of a Small Circle of Friends by Phil Ochs (live in Vancouver 1969)
Trigger Alert : those with technophobia (fear of computers) may want to stop reading (and get off their phones)

I went to add to my facebook profile (most of it is funny and made up as I don't want people to know too much about me like where I live) since it had a space for 'Position'. Now I guess that means like a job and not a favourite position so I didn't write 'doggie'.
To my surprise, facebook made the following suggestions, obviously determined by spying on my posts and friends (stuff in brackets is my added reaction and/or truth) :
1) self - employed : (cross between sort of and I wish)
2) Founder : (or what or everything?)
3) Patient Advocate for cannabis (how did they know?. This can get you suspended and/or banned from facebook. Yes, it's essentially fascist tactics.)
4) Canada Post (not really though before the internet, I'd join the millions waiting for the Friday mail with my Pogie, Employment Insurance check)
5) Master of Social Work (true - how did facebook know that I had this degree when it is never ever mentioned in my digital life)
6) Former Cannabis Rights Coalition (untrue and scary if US customs sees that...this one is most definitely based on an invasion of posts made by my facebook friends)

7) Teacher (true but how did fb know that teacher and social worker come up 1 and 2 on employment tests?)

8) Shining Light Productions (where did this come from?) I had to google this. 'SSL is the standard security technology for establishing an encrypted link between a web server and a browser'.

So basically facebook is somehow providing me with a warm, fuzzy feeling of being secure despite their intrusion to know/guess numbers 1 to 7...

All this despite the rest of my profile about lives in Kathmandu, beard growing and chillums (the chillum part was removed by facebook). Go figure - even intrusion is not always correct (outside a small circle of true friends). So I ended up putting 'Me' as Position...as in being me is my job...

Knowledge of the World in their Hands

Suggested Music : I Can See Clearly Now by Jimmy Cliff (video version)

Trigger Alert: those with sophophobia (fear of knowledge or learning) may want to stop reading.

This came to me during an insomnia night.

When I was 12 to 16 years old, I was forced by circumstances to go to summer camp for the 2 summer months. Transistor radios were a relatively recent invention which meant they were expensive. At this rich kid camp, everyone had one, except me. And the only ones that could get Toronto rock stations were made by Sony. If only I had bought the stock. So now I was thinking that since so many things were invented due to the invention of transistors in 1947, what would it be like if someone time travelled back to 1950 (peak of the Baby Boom)? Let's have TT represent the time traveller and 1950 represent a scientist from that time.

1950 : I see all kinds of possibilities for inventions after transistors are made tiny. I can see how this would make computers smaller, maybe even desk size, maybe even capable of sending messages back and forth.

TT: Well, you are on the right track. There is something called the internet invented in 1983 and now used for a great deal of all communication. But here's one that will surprise you. They are called smart phones, that go anywhere, about the size of your hand, send typed messages and access this internet thing. So with one, a person can look up almost anything in the world.

1950 : That's amazing. That means people have the knowledge of the world in their palms. That will be used for so much advancement. Let me guess. It's the end of war and poverty in the world. The knowledge of the world used for good. So many advancements.

Tell me, tell me, what do people use these smart phones for? I just have to know

TT : Well most people use them for arguing with people on another phone, a person they have never met. Oh, and watching videos, mostly of cats and dogs.

1950 : (speechless)

Spam

Suggested Music : Monty Python Spam Song

Trigger Alert : Those with spamophobia may want to stop reading. Now which kind of spam this refers to pappy doesn't know so pick your own.

We all probably know spam. There are of course 2 main kinds. So let's do both.

1)Spam - the luncheon 'meat'. Came out in 1937 by Hormel. Just in time for the WWII. Even the Russian Army said they would not have been able to feed their army without Spam. And it has that niffy twisty thing to open. I wonder if the Russian troops had Spam cuts from the cans.

Now did you ever wonder what is in Spam (if you haven't ever tried it, you may want to forgo it and use your imagination). Pork, ham meat, salt, water, modified potato starch, sugar, sodium nitrite (so beware those with a nitrite allergy) and gelatin formed when cooking in can (because gelatin is extracted from the skin, bones, and connective tissues of animals such as domesticated cattle, chicken, pigs, and fish - who knew?). A google search for 'gelatin' actually contains the question if gelatin is vegetarian or not...

In case you are rushing out to buy Spam, it's $3.48 a can at Walmars. And if travelling (maybe starving in the desert or 100 meters from the top of Everest), not to worry. Spam is available in more than 100 countries.

2) Spam - those annoying unsolicited messages you get on your computer, phone, ipad, whatever, in the form of an email. It is clear that the term came from the Monty Python skit where the word spam is used a sickening number of times. Now you would figure with email invented in 1971, some early nerd would claim he came up with the word spam at lunch one day or something. But no. No one came forward. And he could have been on the cover of Time like the inventor of email. Or maybe it was someone in Africa with a lot of extra millions to put in your bank just as soon as you divulged your soon to be empty bank account number. One thing for sure, Spam is a fucking technological aggravation. And it ain't going nowhere. Both kinds. There are 20 kinds of spam (food) and who knows how many kinds of email...

Welfare

Suggested Music : Nobody Knows You When You're Down And Out by Nina Simone

Trigger Alert : those with peniaphobia, the fear of poverty, may want to stop reading.

We always called it welfare. Unemployment insurance was 'pogie'. Evidently, there are many slang terms for welfare. Many of them are racist and outrageous but here are some softer ones (I counted about 900 slang terms on google!!!). Some of the less outrageous: beach bum, Doritos day, welfare (followed by various derogatory names), tugboat, white trash, bong drunk, hippie kit.

I had just got back from India. It's hard to cover those years on a resume. 'Staring at the Taj Mahal' doesn't cut it. I applied for welfare, got $50 a month which was my rent in a shared house years ago and they gave me $2 for food. I knew the welfare decision man's assistant but we had to pretend we didn't know each other. Awkward. His boss said about the $2 for food: "you can buy some rice with that". Maybe you think I made this up but you can't make this shit up. I didn't say anything for fear of losing $2 in rice. I obviously had to rely on my roommates for food. The cruel, unnecessary comment was so out of line. I really have no idea why he only gave me $2 for food. At the time, there were no food banks.

The office where you had to pick up the check was only blocks from my mother's house, so I rode my bike the back way. She never knew but probably wondered how I paid my rent. One time, they made us line up so they could offer us a job at the coin mint. The only question asked was (to the 'long hairs') 'are you willing to cut your hair?'. Answering 'yes' got you the job. Answering 'no' I never found out what you got, maybe no rice. I got my hair cut what I saw as short (it was) but they saw it as 'still too long'. The other thing was that it was very noisy stamping out coins. Many workers were deaf or partially deaf. I am now partially deaf because of this as they refused proper ear protection. I later tried to sue but got laughed at and told that it would take at least 5 years to sue and I would likely lose. When I had enough saved, I did the only possible thing : went back to India because who knows what the next 'goodie' would be and it beat getting 'hippie kits'. Besides, $2 could get me quite a few days food in India. Assuming I could somehow get that check, which of course I couldn't. Shit man, if I could have gotten a check I might still be in India.

When you have hash but no implements of ingestion

Suggested Music : Champagne & Reefer by Muddy Waters

Trigger Alert : Those with capnophobia / fumiphobia, fear of smoking, may want to stop reading.

Special Note : hashish is illegal in Canada so of course this is all written in jest...

There are times when you have some hash but seemingly no way to smoke it (no pipe/bong/etc.). Don't panic. Here are some helpful hints from Happy Pappy so you can still get really bald :

1) Poor person's vape.

Required: thumb tack, china plate, medium size clear glass, bendy straw, hash (Red Leb preferred). Place thumb tack on plate, put piece of hash on point of thumb tack, light til smoke turns black, blow out, immediately cover with glass, carefully use bendy straw under edge of glass to inhale. Enjoy.

This is considered a necessary ritual when at a cottage, especially at 4:20. Smoke outs between pairs is the best. Immediately immerse yourself in cold lake water to revive.

2) Apple (the fruit).

Required: apple, knife, pin, tin foil, hollow pen, hash (any kind). Use knife to hollow out core about half way through. Make hole from side to join other hole. Cover first hole with tin foil, use pin to make small holes in tin foil, hollow bic pen makes good extension. Guess the rest. Eating apple after is optional as it may be an acquired taste. Enjoy.

This comes in very handy when hiking as you likely have the required tools but you must remember to pack an apple. It is assumed you will remember the hash.

3) Lunch at the corner in high school (in 1969).

Required: student on lunch at corner, safety pin, bic pen, hash (no kief).

Sit at corner at lunch time. Place hash on pin, discard ink cartridge in bic pen (as you will no longer feel like writing), light hash, inhale with hollow pen. Suck on mint (optional) and do not get caught (important for future educational endeavours). Hire tutor for afternoon subjects (optional). A lost art common in late 1960's. Enjoy.

*Cannabis in Canada (so far) Part 1 (*March 2019)

Suggested Music : I Can See Clearly Now by Jimmy Cliff , written by Johnny Nash from film *Cool Runnings*
Trigger Alert : Those with cannaphobia (fear of cannabis) should stop reading and read reality instead.
Disclaimer: hashish and cannabis edibles are currently illegal in Canada. Therefore, this story includes reference to illegal activities (eg smoking hash) so do not replicate this behaviour.

It started off seemingly well. The previous government had kept their fascist ways by treating medical users worse than dirt by insisting that medical growers put all their grow into the garbage mixed with kitty litter to cut the smell. No one of course did this but the minister of health received a large number of envelopes filled with kitty litter (I never heard if it was used kitty litter...)
But with the new government, the whole legalization path soon started to crumble. The task force was led by an ex-police chief. The reality of so called 'legalization' became clear : collect tax money, give financial control to friends with large corporations, and pass lots of new laws that were all about control. It quickly became delegalization / defined criminalization.
I remember being at the cottage and a friend arriving all excited as there was now a date for legalization. I was less than impressed. We were smoking bud but we were also smoking hash and eating edibles, the hash and edibles would still be

illegal. Our return home was like a yawn. Where we lived had 33 cannabis dispensaries, more than Starsucks and Timmy Hortons. The city was scrambling trying to charge 11 grand for business licenses. The local cops were saying 'hey we got other things to do like the fentanyl deaths'.

But other places were different. Legalized differently with different stores and big busts of dispensaries with many arrests. In BC, it was all over the map. If you lived in one city, some dispensaries slowly died. Other cities, you could be arrested while the cops did a bust.

So in BC, many dispensaries remain and one so called legal store opened. The joke going around was a few people sitting around smoking a joint, and someone said 'they are opening a store in Kamloops, let's go' . The others said 'where the fuck is Kamloops?'

To be continued...Part 2 'how I celebrated legalization, after yawning'. Or 'how the Province hired goons to shut the dispensaries' if that happens as they say they will ...

Cannabis in Canada (so far) Part 2

How I celebrated legalization, after yawning'

Suggested Music : Bang on the Drum by Todd Rundgren, Live at Daryl's House (but live at Todd's house in Maui)

Trigger Alert : Those with cannaphobia (fear of cannabis) should stop reading and read reality instead.

Disclaimer: This story involves cannabis recreational and strictly medical dispensaries, some of which are grey market and hence illegal. I accept no responsibility for your visit or purchase. Reference to shatter is illegal.

Yawn. Not much going on. Some of the 33 dispensaries had faded due to exorbitant business licenses by city (11 grand). Now the big day. Cannabis (dried) becomes legal, you can grow 4 plants (whoopy-do) and be arrested by like 20 something new laws.

So I decided that it would be cool to try to visit every dispensary that day. And I would ride one of the new city free green bikes unlocked by app then leave out for next tourist. Fortunately, uptight Oak Bay didn't allow dispensaries - I was worried cause the green bikes don't come with helmets and Oak Bay confiscates any bike when you don't have a helmet. So off I go with map from Weedmaps, headed to the nearest dispensary (one block). Then back to looking for a green bike (whose program is now failing). No bike, stopped at 2nd dispensary. Made it to 3rd dispensary after finding bike.

Now there were some problems with my road trip. One, I had no idea what to ask. 'High, happy legal day, are you gonna close or be arrested?' That wouldn't do. Two, none of the owners were there. Probably, doing a run, watering the plants or just plain counting money. Three, the staff were all stoned and didn't know what to say. Four, I felt guilt that I wasn't buying at least a gram and 33 stores X average $10 I couldn't afford. And Five, all 3 got me stoned on shatter and I slowly lost interest and went to the beach. I took some sticks and banged on a rock.

To be continued : Part 3 - 'how the Province hired goons to shut the dispensaries' if that happens as they say they will ...

Cannabis in Canada (so far) Part 3 – Narcs wanted

Suggested Music : Legalize It by Peter Tosh
Trigger Alert : those with astynomiaphobia (fear of police) may want to stop reading.

Well if you were just dying to apply as a new 'narc' in BC, here's your chance to prove that legalization is a fake, it's just criminalization in sheep's clothing.
Now they say that cops that don't make it as cops become campus cops and then when they don't make it as campus cops, they become : Administrative Officer 21 – Investigator / Administrative Officer 24 – Senior Investigator (BC)

Now in case this job posting has been taken down, here are some highlights (parts in brackets are my additions):
- part of Ministry of Public Safety and Solicitor General (aka law enforcers who also jail real criminals)
- five years experience in enforcement (think failed cop)
- experience with covert operations and surveillance (think failed cop)
- long periods in poor conditions while carrying out surveillance (think failed cop)
- writing, preparing and organizing search warrants (think failed cop)

- work in locations that may pose a variety of risks/hazards e.g. weapons, drug use, prostitution, organized crime, remote locations, poor weather, etc. (think failed cop with no Tim Hortons)
- helps to be right wing, anti cannabis jerk (I made that one up)

So...if you like busting people like armed criminals, addicts, sex trade workers, mafia, all when stuck in a car on an abandoned road in a blizzard, then this job is not for you. But if you enjoy enforcing unjust laws and depriving medical patients from relief from pain, this is you !!!

Given the severe lack of ability to hire staff for 'illegal' dispensaries, these jobs may be posted for a while. Please note that some areas will be boring as local narcs have already busted these hardened criminals. However, there still remain a number of dispensaries to bust so still lots of fun to have. Especially for failed cops/campus cops.

Note: qualifications are less than required for budristas in legal dispensaries. For example, budristas need criminal record check...

Note: billy clubs and binoculars provided.

Cannabis in Canada (so far) Part 4 - Expensive Hobby

Suggested Music : Didn't I (Blow Your Mind) – *Live at Daryl's House* (but at Todd Rundgren's House in Hawaii)

Trigger Alert – those with botanophobia,fear of plants, or anthophobia, the fear of flowers should stop and completely forget this.

Well, the so called illegal medical dispensaries are all closed as I guess they hired enough goons as mentioned in Part 3. With the transition to government approved dispensaries selling inferior cannabis for high prices, the choices became the BM (black market with lower prices) or the part of 'legalization' where under certain circumstances 4 plants can be grown by households. There are too many flaws in this idea to list. For one thing, unless you happen to be an expert grower of giant plants, 4 plants outside in Canadian summer is not enough for most medical needs or indeed recreational use.

But that is just the beginning as restrictions in the law mean most renters can not grow so you need to own a house (where average prices can start at 1 million). And the house would have to be such that the 4 plants are not visible to the public (whatever that means). So a million dollar house that also has some privacy. Growing inside is risky as most house insurances are voided by this.

So, ok, you have all of the above. It is an expensive hobby. First, you need to prepare the soil (expense), then you generally need to buy clones from the black market (expense) unless you can buy pricey seeds and start the plants inside (again invalidating the house insurance). So you have 4 expensive clones in the expensive dirt in your expensive backyard. Then often add expensive fertilizers and various organic sprays for various bugs as it turns out we are not the only things that love cannabis.

But don't plan on going away as you need to tend the plants every single day (and you're too paranoid to get anyone else). You've got 4 expensive pets that need to be fed. And the closer those flowers get to be ripe, the more chance that molds and bugs can quickly ruin the whole crop. Then there are the thieves. Happens all the time. So you may want to build new fences, gates, motion sensors and cameras and get attack dog (great expenses).

But congratulations. You have 4 ripe plants that you can harvest, dry in rooms with perfect humidity (expense) and then store dried flowers in fancy containers (expense). And remember. You almost certainly don't have enough to last you or your family or friends who rent. So you eventually have to go back to buying in the black market. And you think, shit man, I could just buy from the ever cheaper black market all the time, and fuck that growing 4 plants...which is what the government wants except they blew it in their eyes by making the black market cheaper and popular.

Yay...and fuck you

“We were wondering if you'd like to share”

Suggested Music : Try Jah Love by Third World

Trigger Alert : Those with nosocomephobia, the fear of hospitals, may want to stop reading.

Note : references to illegal smoking hash are strictly 'do not try illegal substances' disclaimer.

It was 1974, fresh back from 2 years travelling in India and Nepal. I was immediately put into a special hospital ward for tropical diseases. Having smoked hash for those 2 years, I called an old buddy who brought me 3 important things: pipe, matches, hash. I figured out the nurse's routine. I knew that the nurse did a 3 am check in, so I pretended to be in dream land. As soon as the nurse left, I opened the window as far as it went and carefully blew smoke out. The nurse was bored maybe as she did another round at which point, I was peacefully staring out said window. Went back to bed, nothing said. I lay there (did I mention how ill I was?) and proceeded to have anxiety and become convinced that I was likely dying in this shitty room with a window that didn't open far enough.

Next morning, doctor rounds. The senior, older doctor and his young up and coming doctor. So before trying to continue to figure out what was wrong with me, the young one said, "The nurse said there were sweet smells in your room last night. Since you are just back from India, we were wondering if you'd like to share some." He wanted a piece of the action. Or bust me right out of the hospital (I unfortunately had to stay to get well). I quickly showed them some bidis as I had to try to explain smell. They went on to about my diagnosis despite clearly not believing me. I had to wait for discharge before getting high again. What a drag...despite my impending death anxiety.

I was discharged after a couple of weeks, went to catch the subway to who knows where. Another man had also been discharged after being in India. He said, "They told me I had a 50/50 chance of survival so to go enjoy". I suddenly felt better as at least I hadn't been told that. I gave him a piece of hash but I still wonder about him now. Though he appeared 'enjoyed'...

My troubled relationship with tobacco

Suggested Music : there is all kinds of 'stop smoking' meditation/subliminal stuff HERE. Take your pick. Stop smoking right now !!!

Trigger Alert : NOT reading this may be hazardous to your health.

I started smoking tobacco at age 16 when I went to high school in Switzerland. Smoked Winston's as they were cheap there and maybe I had fallen for the ads. I immediately quit when I got back as I was living at my Mom's house and she hated smoke. Then at University, I would need tobacco to roll hash joints and it was a small step to smoking some straight tobacco since one needed to buy a pack. But I quit more or less but then when I was 23, I was on the infamous Istanbul to Tehran 4 day train - there was no water, food or anything and it didn't stop. So we brought everything with us but boring it was. We had the compartment locked with a steel bar as people tried to break in every night. But one day we let a Turkish Army General in for his short trip. Turns out that the Turkish army is provided with packs of smokes for about 2 cents a pack (then) and the General had a large bag of the packs which he kindly left us. I started to smoke again. Now they were Turkish tobacco so weren't that bad though very strong and if you dared to open one, it had twigs in it. The bottom of the plant I'm guessing.

Once I got to India, I made the big mistake of switching to beedis (bidis). Now these are like tiny cigars made from some kind of non tobacco leaf stuff with very coarse tobacco inside. About 4 cents for 25 so they were the poor people smoke whereas others indulged in British cigs (another hangover from their rule). This went on for all my 2 years in India/Nepal. Then when I got back, I was so ill that I quit and didn't smoke for a few years again. I'm not sure what happened that got me going again...went back to school, baby on the way, bought a house. I just don't remember the trigger as there always seems to be a stressful one when you go back to smoking. And I discovered that French cigs like Gauloise and Gitane cigs were made in Quebec, and you guessed it, with Turkish tobacco. And I discovered that beedhis were available in Toronto basically illegally in a store back room so black market, no taxes, 20 pack cartons. Now I had just chosen to smoke probably the strongest tobacco I could find. Once our daughter was born I quit. But working at new jobs meant being able to smoke OPs (other peoples) for years. Not many but enough and in binges.

Now here is a way to quit permanently forever but it is **NOT** recommended. I had a stroke. I stood up and was instantly blind in one eye, my good side eye. And despite later finding out that a shot at Emergency would have saved it, I received horrible care at the hospital. The doctor on ignored me and the specialist took 5 hours to get there. There is a max 3 hour window for the shot. I didn't know and they didn't care I guess. Now I only have one eye which has glaucoma (unrelated to stroke) and have a right hand/arm attentional shake. This means reaching or holding anything is difficult and unpredictable. I can drive but it is way more difficult as I have no depth perception. I can't really cook except very basic things. So my life changed dramatically. There is no doubt that the years of smoking good tasting, strong and deadly Turkish tobacco ultimately led to a stroke. Did this example lead to other people I knew to stop? Not really. That friend as well as my daughter eventually but it took years.

But if reading this tilts anyone towards quitting, DO IT NOW. Not later but NOW. Is it easy? No. Is it important? Yes. I worked in a long term rehab retreat for heroin addicts. They all smoked and said if quitting smoking was as easy as quitting heroin then they would have done it...

'Giving up smoking is the easiest thing in the world. I know because I've done it thousands of times.' (Mark Twain)

godfathers, godmothers, godpersons (non binarys etc)

Suggested Music : Hey You by Bachman Turner (live in NYC)
Bonus Music : Volunteers by Jefferson Airplane (live at Woodstock)
Saving Grace [in me] by Todd Rundgren
Trigger Alert : Those with hypengiaphobia (fear of responsibility and accountability) may want to stop reading and get help immediately.

I wrote this with the word 'friend' as it was to be published in a magazine that might end up in the country where a certain person lives. But it was like in a Perry Mason TV show where people using 'friend' meant themselves. But when I heard it was no longer to be published, I decided to make it stronger and more bitter as I no longer cared.

Godfathers, Godmothers, Godpersons. I hope that covers all possibilities for this very special being. That's the word - 'being'. It says it all. This a story about our child's godparents .It was/is my story, it is almost too painful to write or even think. A trust and a betrayal. Not real godparents as they abdicated all responsibility in an unexplained, very painful way.

Why would we choose such slouches? Because trust as they say is 'more than telling a stranger your life story'.

When our child was born, we asked our best friends (a couple) to be godparents. They willingly accepted as they were our best friends and he most definitely was my best friend. We had gone on a wild 10 day hike in the Northwest Territories, over glaciers, through roaring rivers, past polar bears.

Then they moved to a foreign country as he was on the verge of being a world famous professional. And years later they split up after having their own child. I noted that we were not asked to be godparents. I didn't say it or even think of it at the time but 'fuck you' comes to mind. Around the same time, I was going through the worse crisis of my life (next to the death of my father when I was 11). I had lost my job and career by being fucked around by another so called 'friend'. I had gone from a good salary to zero on a Friday afternoon. I was hurting and so was my family, including of course our child with the so called godparents. I would chat with my friend as chat on computers had just been invented. One day he seemed to take offence to the fact that we owned a house so had equity but I was broke and on the verge of losing the house. I still have no idea what his problem was as he makes a fortune. That was the end. He never contacted me again and ignored all my attempts to contact him. The most painful part was his godchild now needed a good godfather, but he also ignored them despite genuine attempts by them to contact him in their best very kind, thoughtful way.

So the moral of the story is be very careful whom you pick as godparents.

Oh and one more thing...Fuck you godfather for being an asshole...and I do hope you read this. I might mail it to you on my deathbed.

written without prejudice in case this ever reaches the foreign country they live in...bottom of the muddy barrel trust.

Now, roll the credits…

BONUS: ***David Sedaris Masterclass Submissions:***

Partly because of the pandemic, I thought since I'd have more time to write (not true) so I joined the celeb program called Masterclass where they get celebs in many subjects to provide lessons with accompanying videos. I only joined the one from David Sedaris because I thought it would generate stories. Much like what I wrote for the proposed magazine. It's an expensive course so I was hoping for the best...but no. I think they should have waited until the pandemic so David might have more time. What he provided was great but way too little. Shit, when he lives in England, he probably spent more time in a day picking up garbage on his road (he does this as well as writing every day). Also, the promised (by Masterclass) sense of a community of writers was sorely absent. It just takes one borderline personality disorder to ruin your day and/or the course.

But before dropping out and wasting money, I did most of the 'Assignments' provided by David. Here are some that I did.

Hey, Hey We're the Covidiots (Sing-along)

To the Tune of 'Theme from the Monkees TV show' aka Hey, We're the Monkees

Here we come,
Walkin' down the street
We get the funniest looks from ev'ry one we meet
Hey, hey, we're the Covidiots
And people say we fuck them around
But we're too busy ignoring
And putting anybody down
We go wherever we want to
Do what we like to do
We don't have time to care
There's always something new
Hey, hey, we're the Covidiots
And people say we fuck them around
But we're too busy trumping
And putting anybody down
We're just plain being stupid
Come and watch us fuck you around
We're the fucked generation
And we've got nothing to say
Any time, Or anywhere
Just look over your shoulder
Guess who'll be standing there

Hey, hey, we're the Covidiots
And people say we fuck them around
But we're too busy pissing
And putting anybody down
Hey, hey, we're plain stupid
And people say we fuck them around
But we're too busy trumping
And putting anybody down
We're just plain being stupid
Come and watch us fuck you around
We're the fucked generation
And we've got nothing to say
Hey, hey, we're the Covidiots
Hey, hey, we're the Covidiots
Hey, hey, we're the Covidiots
You never know where we'll be found
So you'd better get ready
We're already in your town

Assignment : Beards

Write about an event that divided your life into "before" and "after."

Suggested Music : *Reelin' in the Years* by Steely Dan
Kiss on My List by Hall and Oates (live)

I've never written about when my Dad died. I think I still called him Daddy. I've told a few therapists for sure. I went to find his grave many years later. I phoned the cemetery to find the plot so I told them the date he died. I got the month right but was 2 years off. It seemed the cemetery was use to mistakes/guesses.

He was a Supreme Court Justice. One Friday after work, he said he hadn't felt well at all walking to his car. On Sunday in the middle of the night, I was woken up and told that he was asking for me. He was lying down and kissed me and said goodbye. I was 11 years old (I checked) and had no idea what to do so I went back to bed and fell asleep. Later my Mother's scream woke me up. He had died of a heart attack. I think he was 51.

We had 2 cottages at the time and the summer before we had spent a while at his favourite. We would canoe out to a small island but one day, we tipped near shore. As my Daddy struggled to right the canoe, I sat on shore feeling totally helpless. The same helpless as when I knew he had died.

But during that vacation, he grew a beard just for that time. I don't think he had ever done that before. It was red. I was amazed by the colour. My beard was initially reddish. His last summer was a happy one except for the canoe.

Now at my brother's cottage (he has 2 cottages too). My family never spoke about Father after he died. Never. But 50 years later, my brother and I were talking about him. I was again sitting on a shore but without a tipped canoe. Another summer, before my Dad died my family had taken a cruise ship along Lake Superior. That boat no longer exists. We were on our way to pick up my brother who had a summer job somewhere on the lake. And he had grown a beard. My father was very displeased and insisted it be shaved off immediately. My brother says father was strict but I can tell you as the baby in the family he was never strict with me in the slightest way. My brother was clearly fascinated by my story of the red beard. He checked my memory. Could this be his father who had freaked out about his beard. My brother and I get along well, maybe because I only see him once a year as his cottages are just down the beach from mine. He semi laughingly pointed out how disapproving my Father would be of my very long beard. I could only agree and wonder to myself about life if he had not died. Somehow I did not see myself with a beard. Somehow.

Assignment: Dear diary

'Using one of the three humour tools that David employs regularly, write about watching a stranger and quickly understanding how cheap he is.'

Recovering in bed so no edits after. Wondering about the course. I've done all the assignments i was comfortable with – mixed results. Some i really liked, nobody in class noticed or didn't get to them. One in particular. So i sent it to my most ardent, brutal critic – my daughter – she loved the piece. So i thought maybe i'd stop the course though when I'm not writer blocked, it was a relief writing. I even told my counsellor that. Anxiety would go. But Something changed and I don't know what. Now I feel anxious, apprehensive about posting anything. I feel it in my gut, like there's a test coming up in high school.

So then after considerable deliberation, i think i'll do some of the rest of the assignments but really stretch the idea if needed. Why? Cause that's the best way to not give a shit. Will i write and post every day? Nah. Will i read other posts more – probably – will i comment on posts...highly unlikely. If the anxiety doesn't lessen then I plan to drop the course. So here goes.

(end of diary)

He cheap, she cheap, me cheap

So this is a real fuckin stretch. The only part I think I use is the word 'cheap'

So basic question is David Sedaris cheap? I don't know what cheap means. Is it the opposite of generous? If so, then he was generous. Was. For example, in the past, small towns would be picked to have someone read Santaland Diaries at Xmas time for free. And David would do a reading and signing at bookstores for free.

But it is an enigma. I was at a reading of David's and someone asked about his brother Rooster and David said 'I don't talk to him now as he owes me money'. Then there is his story of the last time he saw one of his sisters before she committed suicide. All he did was have the door slammed on her.

But then again, he bought the family the summer house on the beach that they always visited in the past. That's not cheap.

So just for fun, I did a google search where it says what a person is worth (money wise). Now how these are arrived at, who knows. Says David is worth 8 million. Somewhat surprisingly Amy Sedaris is richer at 10 million. So why didn't she spring for the beach house? She used to be generous as when everything on her table at home was always on sale for 25 cents. Now?...She was just on late night TV from her craft room. She was taking pieces of thread and rabbit hair from a jar, gluing them onto tongue depressors and wanted $10 each. Suddenly seemed like a rip off.

Am I cheap? Absolutely. Otherwise, I would have been homeless and starving long ago. Instead, I'm anxious about writing for a course that I thought was expensive.

PS : Amy : I'll take 10 of those tongue depressors...

***Assignment** : Write a story in the form of a letter* **Letter to David Sedaris**

Little, Brown and Company,

1290 Avenue of the Americas,

New York, NY 10104

Dear David:

I liked it when you came to the bookstore to read and sign books, all for free. The first time here I think it was 8 people showed up but then second time, the space was full with people in the hall. You read your story Nicaragua about your teacher. It worked so well verbally but not for print. We still pronounce it that way...

Now I see you're coming back to Victoria and Vancouver as you did last year. Sadly, we can't afford the tickets. Sadly, the free days are gone...

Here's my story part. When we met you, my spouse immediately made a comment about your astrological signs. She always does this, often getting guesses right though this time she knew you were a Capricorn. You said something like 'oh, i don't follow that stuff'.

You and I talked about having a friend in common. Kathie, Spalding Gray's widow. You actually thought she was still your theatrical agent which I found hilarious given that she probably hadn't been for years.

Another friend of ours was back in the lineup. As she came to you, you looked at her, told her her sun sign, rising sign and moon (all correctly) and that my friend has a black cat (she did). We tried to get you sushi but everything was closed.

Then my friend (with the black cat) came to my cottage to visit and I had just gotten *Calypso* the day it came out. You said in one of the stories how you would sometimes make up things about people in line and then tell them. And sometimes you are correct, by chance (I assume). So I read her that passage from the book. She insisted there must be more to it. I said Amy wouldn't have paid big bucks for that psychic about Tiffany if all she had to do was ask you...

So David, here are the chances (probability) that you randomly guessed my friend's signs correctly. 1 out of 12 x 1/12 x 1/12 = 1 chance out of 1728 (or a probability of about .05787)... (I'll give you the black cat guess cause looking at her, even I would have probably got that right ...)

So really good guess, David...

ps : give my best to Amy

pps: thanks for the Masterclass

ppps: (let Kathie know when the comp tickets are at the box office – Victoria). I will bring my family doctor as he is a huge fan of yours. He worked for decades as an Emergency Room doctor so will have lots of weird medical stories you will enjoy.

John Boland,Victoria, BC, Killaloe, ON

(Bali/Phuket, Poste Restante address added to Masterclass version)

Assignment – 'Write about an event that divided your life into before and after.'

Trigger warning – use of the work 'fuck' as in 'fucked around'.
Suggested Music : *She (fucking) Hates Me* by Puddle of Mud
There is a series of incidents that changed my life forever. It has changed my life and my family's life this week – this very day. Everyday. It is the reason I have symptoms of PTSD. I know that tonight when I can't sleep as every night for over 20 years has been, I will know it is these incidents. My friend calls them 'cluster fucks' when you get fucked around time after time about the same thing. But I CAN NOT write about it. If I did, I would be telling the truth but if certain people read it (the people who fucked me around), I might get sued. I have handled this to a certain extent by writing detective fiction where their identity is well hidden but they usually get fucked around and often die in the story. So as much as I would love to hammer them by name, I can't...But safe to say : FUCK YOU ...
The closest I think I can come is 2 stories about bandits I've met. Because the fuckers mentioned above stole my life but are not these bandits. Note that the bandits in the first story were really, really bad to me but the second set of bandits were nice to me (but not necessarily to others). My apologies if these stories are repeats from earlier in this book.

Places not to sleep (Spanish jails)

Two days out of Barcelona, hitchhiking hadn't been bad or great. I had been with 2 women I met and that made getting a ride easier. We had even gotten a ride with a man who let us use his apartment. I hadn't got to fuck them but had arranged to meet them in Morocco, maybe I was dreaming of sex when we'd be smoking Moroccan kief. But alas the next day, they got a ride by themselves and my soon to be desperate situation meant I never caught up so we could meet in Morocco. I was now halfway down the Spanish Gold Coast, still heading to Morocco. It was late in the day as I got let out in a lonely section of country. I could see the clouds were dark, ominous and it was getting dark quickly. I know from sleeping in the ditch by Golden, BC that this is not advisable at all. It's not comfortable and dreams in a ditch can be nightmares.

A Mercedes (Mercenary Bents) stopped. Two Germans guys in black leather pants. Alarm bells were going off but I ignored them. They stopped at a bar in nowheresville and we drank a lot of cognac. I have to say as much as I like cognac, I never drank it again. We got going but not for long. The driver guy got out to pee at a pull over but I think he forgot to pee as he came back with a very large gun with what kinda looked like a silencer. They wanted everything. Traveller's checks, passport, cash, my pack. And after all that as I managed to get out of the car, they said it was time to shot me. At that split moment, the aforementioned ditch to sleep in way back there seemed very desirable...

Sleeping in the Khyber Pass (Do Not Sleep in Landi Kotal)

There's so much more to this story as good karma and bodhisattvas saved me but has little to do with bandits (except when the Chief of Police identified them and described how awful dying in a Franco Spanish jail was...). Maybe I'll write about the good karma some day.

The Khyber Pass is a strategic pass between Afghanistan and Pakistan.
Note (for legal purposes) : This area, including Landi Kotal, is no longer safe in anyway so travel there is extremely dangerous and not recommended.

Trigger alert: For once there is none as a fear of bandits is apparently a good thing. But the thing was I had met much worse bandits...

I was going through the Khyber Pass alone by local bus. My female partner had bought a ticket on the direct bus but neglected to buy me one before it sold out. I guess she didn't want to play house anymore. The term 'local bus' that I took is relative as after the first mini bus, the transportation changed to backs of large trucks with the goats and chickens. After a myriad of villages and trucks, I arrived at the Afghan/Pakistan border, a place called Landi Kotal. If you look on the web, even Wikipedia has it listed as a 'tourist' stop. Even then and certainly now, this is a bad and dangerous joke. One site even says the 'adventurous tourist' could tour the hashish factory and the next door factory that made AK47 replicas, solely with blacksmith fires. Dangerous advice.

The large billboard at the border said 'Do Not Stay Overnight in Landi Kotal'. Kind of a hint. Take it as real.

This whole area had a fancy name but it basically meant that there was no government and no police. It was run by bandits. Now maybe the name 'bandit' was a bit harsh. They didn't really seem to steal at random but had it institutionalized. Soon after the 'bus' left the border to go to Pakistan, the bandits had a roadblock. All everyone had to do was pay a toll of exactly what the bus company charged for the trip. The thing was of course, the bandits didn't have expenses such as gas and buses.

So these were rich bandits. When not on roadblock duty, they just hung out in outdoor cafes, armed with AK47 replicas, in part waiting for some Westerner dumb enough to take local buses. All they wanted to see was what happened when you took their offered toke off a huge hookah. Now these hookahs were filled with a bunch of really bad tobacco as well as about 10 grams of hash. The entertainment value was when said Westerner coughed like never before as I staggered to the next cafe. Note that soon after, the Russians invaded Afghanistan which totally pissed off these bandits and given that they already had AK47s, most of them became the Taliban (and no longer were friendly). Thanks, Russia...

I made it through the pass with less and less bandit sightings. By that time, I had forgiven my female travelling partner for abandoning me but she was nowhere in sight. No Hallmark movie happy ending here.

Assignment: 'choose a short piece you've written and write it again in a new way...'

Stroke

Ok so I'm going to tell this true story that isn't very happy. Then I'm going to give it a happy ending. Will this alleviate any ptsd left from the incident? Maybe. I doubt it.

Story (true version) :

I stood up to leave a friend's place. I was suddenly, immediately blind in my right eye (my good eye). I was confused, maybe in shock. I thought, oh well, there's something in my eye and I'll go home and have my partner look at it. When I got home, we decided that I should get a ride to Emergency. Discovered on the way that driving in the dark with one eye is a major challenge. I discovered what no depth perception does.

I got to the hospital...but I missed a cardinal rule. You get better, faster treatment and triage when you get an ambulance. Turns out a lack of doctors meant that there was only an intern on, and the eye specialist took 5 hours to show up. Now neither pointed out that I probably had had a stroke. I had. And they didn't mention that if they worked fast I could get a certain injection and save my eye. Instead the intern said 'I have real emergencies to take care of' and then sent me home. My right eye never came back and I am now blind in the right eye, have no depth perception, can't write and struggle to feed myself due to a tremor.

Now the happy version : I stand up at my friends and my eye seems to bother me a little bit but having read all about the symptoms of strokes (look them up !!!), I called 911 for an ambulance. I got to the hospital and the doctor on turned out to have worked there for years, immediately identified the problem, got me a cat scan immediately, gave me the needed shot and suddenly my eyesight returned. So I got the 'message' and lost a bunch of weight, lowered my blood pressure and cholesterol and lived happy ever after cooking and feeding myself. Man, was I lucky...

Family ('nough said)

“Here’s a challenge for your quarantined writer’s block.”

Continue any piece starting with this sentence:

As he pushed open the door, trying not to let its creaking unsteady his nerves, he saw the message on the floor.”

Virus : pandemic is close to pandemonic is close to pandemonium, just ask Pan

I left it there to dry. I felt like I should step on it and then my one red footprint across the floor would look like a monster had been by. Again, thank the gods that I didn't but stepping on the pandemic had a temptation built in.

On the counter was a note, done in red finger paint. Nice touch.

'get over it. you can now write about your family. Not the live ones stupid - - - the dead ones ...they can't sue...'

So here it is, the main family that I can write about. My mom and dad are long passed on so I'll leave them out. It's my 2 aunts, my father's older sisters. One, Aunt Dorothy was an angel who treated me like royalty. So did her husband, Uncle Carl. When Uncle Carl graduated from law school, it must have been in the 20s, he got a job with a new company called AT&T which since brand new had little money so paid my Uncle half salary, half stock. As a result, he became very wealthy and they retired early in a country estate outside of NYC. Aunt Dorothy was a Grand Master in Bridge, not an easy thing to become (think Omar Sharif) so they travelled the world, she playing bridge and he playing golf. At some point, Uncle Carl died and Dorothy moved to Florida since her sister lived there. The other aunt, marie. But marie was a psychopath. Over the years, she manipulated Dorothy and through a hell that is painful to think about let alone write, she stole the AT&T stock that Dorothy lived on but was also destined to go to us in her will. I would have gotten enough money to buy at least 3 houses in a location I knew would be valuable years later. Now they would be worth more than 3 million $s. As life turned out, my lovable Aunt Dorothy died and aunt marie, whom I hated with a passion, lived far too long. I think Dorothy is somewhere as a Bodhisattva and marie was reborn as a worm...

So there you go. I can write tons about my dead relatives. Does it help? Me? No...

Co(nona)vi(rus)d(isease) – (20)19

(written at the beginning of covid – my, how things change)

Trigger alert : those with mysophobia, also known as verminophobia, germophobia, germaphobia, bacillophobia and bacteriophobia, a pathological fear of contamination and germs may want to stop reading

Bonus video : corona virus prevention video from Vietnam (worth watching)

"everything is funny eventually, sometimes it takes a while , the day will come when you are able to laugh about anything"

Well in the first video of this class, David Sedaris says the above. I would love to write about my family in this context and try to laugh but am unwilling to jeopardize my daughter's benefits from a complex inheritance trust (run by the family).

So I picked the virus. I had already laughed about it so that made it easier. How could I laugh about this? It just happened, kinda like the virus.

I have a friend and for some reason on social media we got into comparing the latest news about the virus. We started this early in the game so there is always lots of 'breaking news'. It came down to who could be the first to tell the other the latest shocking news.

So I did a 'David' and tried this story on a friend. She laughed and asked questions. So although I'm writing here, I am transcribing my verbal story. Helps.

One day recently, we had been comparing what we knew. The latest country to get the virus. Was it in Africa yet as the WHO seemed to think we were more likely fucked in a pandemic when countries got the virus with no medical care or with sanctions. Now I had prepared myself here by asking my brilliant doctor (he graduated early as he skipped 2 grades in high school and one year of med school !!!). He said he would be more concerned if there was suddenly person to person transmission where the victim had not been travelling or in contact with someone say just back from China. Yup, sounded reasonable.

So of course this happened soon after i talked to him in some country far far away. So my friend wrote me 'that's what your doctor said'. But then I got him good. He works late hours so has naps on the weekend. Smokes some indica cannabis (hey, we are in Canada) and goes down for a few hours.

In the 3 hours, I had 3 breaking news for him :

BC where we live had 3 new cases

The US had it's first death

and a dog in some far away country (phew) had it.

If we were keeping score I was now ahead of him. He pointed out how the dog thing didn't really get much news time and at best was minimized like this was no big deal. But the news itself we thought scored him a lot of points. Maybe we were tied now.

So I thought I'd write this. I tried to figure out how to make this an Assignment in the course. But with no luck. You can't make this shit up (exaggeration).

But just now, I just came from the news :

- BC had a huge increase in cases today
- US announced that they would not have enough medical supplies. This almost sounded like surprising truth but then I realized it was just a cover for why they couldn't (wouldn't) send anything remotely humanitarian to say South Korea and good heavens not Iran.
- And a dog in South Korea was placed in quarantine (and where had the dog been?)

I wonder if he's online. This should get me ahead again.

Oh no. He just told me how North Korea is handling people who test positive. They are shot...

I may have solved the writer's block.

This is assuming I make it to the end of 'stay home' phase of the world.

Let's review : David Sedaris has writing offices in 5 places :

1) Sussex and London England – I've been to England a couple of times. It's alright. My problem is that a person who used to be my best friend but abandoned me (very painful) lives in England and there is a chance that I might run into him and a bigger chance that I might seek him out and hire a torpedo.

2) Paris and New York – I love them both, been there multiple times so writing there in a quaint office with a roll top desk and a view – yes, David, I don't know how I knew but you have a roll top desk, don't ya?

3) Emerald Isle, NC – I had to look this up as I have no fucking idea where it is but it sounds nice and I got google maps on my phone so I can drive there if the border ever reopens.

Now, the solution. There is a juice bar place, I can't remember what it's called but it's a chain of them. They said they never had to scout new locations as they would just see where Starsucks was and get a store as close as possible, preferably like next door. So I'm just going to buy 5 offices, each next to David's and if I get bored, or run out of garbage to pick up or get writer's block, I'll just move to another office. Problem solved. Thanks David.

Past, Present, Future (a Repeat in the book but I like it…)

Trigger alert : If you have any or all of the following phobias, you may want to stop reading (especially so if you have all of them !)

1) past - atychiphobia (fear of failure likely based on past failures)

2) present - chronophobia (fear of the passage of time) is the closest fear to match fear of present

3) future - chronophobia - same as fear of present - go figure, go get therapy

Now for a further breakdown:

Past:

Suggested video : Mr. Peabody and Sherman original episodes (24) - pick one

Now wouldn't most (all?) of us want a Way Back Machine in our house. Maybe in the kitchen so it's really handy. Maybe with an app for that, in case you are stuck somewhere.

The biggest problem is figuring out what to change. There are so many things. That mark in grade 5...You'd need to make a long list which would cause the Way Back Machine to malfunction, increasing the likelihood of needing a way back. Be mindful of the past. Or is it be unmindful of the past.

Present :

Suggested music : Reelin' in the Years by Steely Dan

This one is SO easy to stay in the present. Google yoga and see how many types there are. Google meditation and see how many paths there are. So the only question is why are you sitting here, reading this tripe when you could be 'sitting on a cushion' in Kyoto...

Future :

Suggested music / video : guess what it is, using the below mentioned suggestions...

Take the past and present, heat in a beaker, shake well and pour.

Presto : the future.

Oh if it was so easy. Well apparently, it is. Here are some ways to predict the future. Pick one and google it. I take no responsibility for the results.

Psychics, I Ching, Tarot, Astrology, Sabian Symbols, Biorhythms...

Did I miss any? It said I would...

We knew it was coming

When our daughter was little, we took her to a local church for a coop day care. We knew the question was coming. Sure enough after a month or so, one of the women in charge asked my spouse if she would be interested in coming to their church on Sunday. As in a sort of quid pro quo.

Answer:

'Well my mother is Jehovah Witness, my father is Christian Science and my husband is a Buddhist... So I'm basically taken.'

We were never asked about religion again.

Writer's Block

I was asked by a well known college in the US to write something/anything for their blog. I came up with 2 possibilities :
a) PTSD (Part Time So Depressed) but instead when I started to write, my ptsd depression got full timeish OR
b) writer's block.

I never wrote anything as I had been trying to finish my third book for almost 10 years so how the fuck was I going to write for this blog.
So I'll write this here as I realize that I am craving anything remotely like a comment. That's my first mistake. I expect people to find something worth commenting on. The second one is the biggee : expecting someone to appreciate and even enjoy what I write.

From Wikipedia : “The condition was first described in 1947 by Austrian psychoanalyst Edmund Bergler, who described it as being caused by oral masochism, mothers that bottle fed and an unstable private love life.” So let me see. OMG, I'm an oral masochist (bite my nails), my mother's doctor told her to leave me to the bottle and actually...yes...leave (abandon) me with someone else, and I can't comment on my love life, can I as it's private. So maybe it's all these things and I've been going to the wrong therapist. And I thought it was just wanting to fucking get published...

Note : 3 of my favourite authors had writer's block. Dashiell Hammett, J.D. Salinger and Janwillem Van de Wetering. Though I've heard that J D was writing a lot but in secret. And Janwillem never finished what he told me would be the culmination of his detectives as he passed into the Bardo too soon. So don't delay...

ps : Please now that I am in isolation from the virus, please, please can my writer's block please fuck off and can someone publish that 'lost' Salinger...

Assignment : *Being the Plaza*

"Think back to one observation or nt you wrote about in your diary."

Suggested Music : *Earth* by Seals and Crofts (first album)

I don't keep a diary. So the diary police can now come and lock me up. But I do tend to tell stories, some of which I've written down. I like meeting new people as they haven't heard the same story repeatedly. The expression is 'my memory is good, it's just a little short'. So here is a story I tell and maybe it will drift into another area like the assignment actually calls for. The story happened before everything closed and getting groceries became a huge challenge. I remember when all you had to do was come up with the money.

I had a stroke years ago and among other things, lost sight in one eye. I therefore have no depth perception for 20 feet. This makes many things difficult including driving and in particular parking. So I have one of those handicap signs that hang from your rear view mirror so I get to park in the reserved handicap spots. Now, I am like most people and am pissed off when people abuse these spots, usually young males who have no morals but do have a friend who is just running into the beer store for a second. However, this one day that I went to the local plaza, I was confronted by a rude man after I got out of the car.

It is not obvious that I am handicapped as my eye does everything including stinging in the shower and producing tears when I am crying, but does not see at all. So my gorgeous baby blues don't give me away. However, I didn't appreciate being confronted that day so I explained nicely to this man that I was blind in one eye and that meant I could buy one of these handicap parking things and display it. He said he was amazed that being blind in one eye would qualify me. He obviously thought I was lying. So this is what I said to him:

'Well, I'll tell you what to do. Drive home and make an eye patch then come back and try parking.' (I was only serious in a passive aggressive way as even him driving this way would be dangerous as believe me, it's like learning to drive all over with one eye). 'After you get back and park, if you still think I should not qualify for the special parking spot, or think I am perhaps lying, then the plaza manager's office is over there (I pointed) or maybe you would prefer to call the police. But when they arrive, I will be in the grocery store or hardware store if they would like to speak to me'. I then smiled an impish smile and blinked with my blind eye. I didn't wait for anything further from the asshole but maybe should have as it might make the story better. But the blink really was a nice touch.

Now because this involves the local plaza, it reminds me of another impish thing I've done there. But first, I have to put both the plaza and me in perspective. The plaza is in a very wealthy area of one of the wealthiest areas of Canada. So the clientele in the grocery store are mostly yuppies, retired or otherwise. BMWs (Break My Windows) and Mercedes (Mercenary Bents) are considered boring. It's more about how many full size Teslas or Maseratis you see. You get the drift. We call the people yuppie zombies as they aimlessly seem to wander in the parking lot oblivious to almost being run over. And then there is me. Many, many years ago, I decided I was no longer going to cut my hair or my beard. So my hair is thick and very long, way down my back and my beard is very bushy and white. At xmas, young children often point me out to their parents as 'Santa'. I thank them and tell them Santa is on break.

The basic idea being that I don't fit in with the yuppie customers. Inside the grocery store, I stand out I guess. Watching the David Sedaris videos in this course has helped me realize how much I relish this distinction (even though I want the hell out of here to move to a nearby island that is basically run by old hippies). One thing that happens in the store is I get stared at. I've gotten so I kinda time the stares. If I feel it is prolonged and I don't know the person (I tend to avoid people as I have enemies that I dread seeing), then this is what I have been known to do: I approach them in a gentle, no threatening manner (this is hard as I look threatening to them I'm sure) and I say 'It's ok Ma'am/Sir, I'm in a cult and they won't let me cut my hair'.

I think now I'll add a wink of my blind eye. It might as well be good for something. But wouldn't it be great if the man from the handicap parking story was the one staring in the store and I got to start telling him all about the cult, just before winking at him...

Assignment: *Mommy, who is the queen?*

“Think back to one observation or moment you wrote about in your diary. Pick one you liked and remember well. Is there another incident from your life—a memory, an event, a milestone—that is tangentially related to the diary entry in some way? Find a way to link a vignette from your diary to something larger and more meaningful to you, then work to flesh out that diary entry into a full essay.”

Suggested Music : Boy Scout Song Parody by Green Day Original version : Time of your Life (Good Riddance) by Green Day

I know the Assignment calls for stuff from my Diary. Small problem, I don't have a diary. But if I had written this in a diary, it might have been like this. (not quite a full essay yet). I remembered the stories because I had read about the Boy Scouts going bankrupt. I call it the Union Carbide 'solution' to being sued. They killed thousands in India in a chemical explosion in 1984 but got out of settlements by going bankrupt and changing corporate names. The Boy Scouts were going to have to pay out huge settlements over cases of sexual abuse perpetrated by Scout 'leaders'. And I knew a great deal about the subject because for 4 years of my time as a therapist, the clientele were all violent men, most of whom had been abused as children and often sexual abuse.

Diary entry :

It was embarrassing and awkward. I was stuck. Best to just shut up and finish lunch. I am in the lunchroom at work (a rare occurrence as I was usually expected to work through lunch). I had watched a really good documentary the night before on PBS about the Boy Scouts history and founder Baden-Powell. The basic subject was about how Baden-Powell was a fascist and a supporter of Hitler. That although Hitler banned Boy Scouts, he used it as a guide for setting up Hitler Youth. The FBI considered him as a possible Nazi spy. Well, there was a jerky psychologist that I didn't know (but could tell he was a jerk) at the lunch table. Yup – turns out he is a Scout Leader. He was offended and I'll leave it at that. Enough thoughts of my former clients.
Diary entry ends.

Full disclosure : I was never a boy scout nor wanted to be. I did get a camp badge for lighting a fire and boiling water way before I discovered in the Farmer's Almanac the right way to light a fire. So later when our daughter wanted to go to Girl Guides as that was what her friends did, I reluctantly agreed with some trepidation but sincere hope that a girl born on International Women's Day might pick up any hints of sexism.
Even better! She came home after and immediately asked : 'Mommy, who is the queen?' (Singing God Save the Queen was still a mandatory start at Guide meetings then.)

Our immediate Answer :

'Well honey, Aretha is the Queen and Elvis is the King'.

She never went back...

Assignment Page 14 : *'Think of a series of questions to ask strangers throughout your day. Experiment.'*

Suggested Music : One on One by Hall and Oates (live)

It's safe to say that after 2 months of self isolation, I haven't met many strangers. I haven't even seen the grocery delivery person (brave soul deserves a medal) from a distance. I could yell things like 'do you like your job? Do you meet any nice people? Made any new friends?' He's probably fortunate that most people wait for them to be long gone before venturing out the door to pick up the grocery bags before spraying them.

The local free newspaper has a contest every year where people vote online for their favourite things – restaurants, fish and chips, LGBTQ (did I miss a letter) bars, nude lakes (there's only one official one so that's a shoe in) etc. One of the categories is 'best place to meet new people'. This of course is a euphemism for 'pick ups'. A certain local grocery store always wins. Amazing as it leaves online dating far behind. Me, I go there in the past BV (Before Virus) and walk/shop the fastest I can go. I think once or twice I have met people who seem nice or at least will respond when I say something. I don't see extolling the good of tempeh as an attempted pick up. Generally though the yuppies and hipsters that can afford to shop there either ignore me or better still frown. It may be my looks of being an old hippie who for some reason can afford to shop there. I may have written before about relishing stares that if they last long enough I tell them 'it's ok I'm in a cult'.

But this is all before now. Just yesterday, some restaurants and such were allowed to open with less tables with mandatory staff masks etc. But me, still paranoid, see that the only people on the news going these places are not people I want to meet or even be more than 6 feet away from. They look exactly like the people who ignored the restrictions anyway. But back to thinking about that grocery store where pick up supposedly means more than groceries, they have taken out part of the street so that people can have more room to line up and have painted circles where you are allowed to stand, letting in 10 shoppers at a time. So how can I brave myself down there and ask strangers questions? First I'd probably have to yell as a surprisingly number of the rich retired yuppies are hard of hearing. And of course I have to be asking strange questions.

I would have to go down there before 7 am (special hour for seniors and disabled like we get up that early...) and wait to be the second in line so I would have a chance at yelling at the first person in line. Here are some possible strange questions.

'Been here long? Been to Disney? The lineups are shorter.'

'Did you get to sleep last night or just wait til 7 am?'

'I just had my virus test but the results aren't for a few days. Does that concern you?'

'Is that a real Maserati?'

'Have you ever picked up a new 'friend' in the tofu aisle?'

I'll let you know the resulting answers.

Assignments Masterclass: People I Hate (aka fuck you Miss Pinch)

I really have a hard time with this section. I've written before about how hard it is to write about my family or certain very negative things that have happened to me when I worked as a Professional. (So I wrote at some point about my dead Aunts as they can't sue.) I won't even say what degrees I have (2 undergrad and a Masters). I once wrote on my web page about a member of my family in a humorous way – they haven't spoken to me since and have been I'd say nasty. To write about my profession might end me up in court being sued.

So I don't feel comfortable doing some of these assignments plus I'm having a lot of anxiety about the virus as I am medically high risk and in self isolation for a month so far. But I did realize that I probably wouldn't give a kidney to anyone (Assignment 3), besides I'm too old and my kidneys aren't great.

However, as things will be, I had just finished a story that almost perfectly fits Assignment 4 (Page 24) :

'Write a scene about a cruel teacher whom you loved or a kind teacher whom you hated.' Except it's a cruel teacher I hated.

Suggested Music : She (fucking) Hates Me by Puddle of Mudd (live)

Oh, I read that hate is a bad word or at least negative. Yup. Sure is. But I'll use self-isolating as my excuse.

I won't write much about the bosses I hate, mostly because some are likely alive. Some I certainly wish were not alive. A couple I've put a curse on so hopefully that worked though google doesn't list any of them as having a memorial service or anything. But maybe the curse also...nah. Let me see, count the bosses I hated (I did have one or two good ones). I get 8 off the top of my head. I know one had the agency funding pulled and 2 got fired so that's good. Sadly one of the good ones died. How unfair is that...

So I'll write about a really early hate. Grade 5 teacher, Miss Pinch. Given her age, I'm sure she's dead and given her everything else no one would have married her so there's no estate to sue me. She was ugly as sin – I have no idea what that expression means but she was very ugly, very nasty. She also was a bully. She would pick on one person at a time and eventually send them to the principle for some lame reason.

I made a mistake. When it was speech time, we had to do a 2 minute speech on any topic. I wish I could have talked about bullies. I did a good stand up job of how to not do a good speech. I had the shakes down pat and other common mistakes. Everyone liked it but her. She picked on me for quite a while before I ended up with the principle. I think he knew as he didn't really do anything. But I got a bad taste of being bullied which has defined different parts of my life. So Miss Pinch, even if you were reborn as a worm that got pierced by a hook and eaten by a fish, fuck you and I fucking hate you...

Assignment (unofficial) – call it 'stuck in writer's block' or 'desperate entry from middle of night diary assignment '

I'll post this though I liked it more when I wrote it. I'm terribly stuck, feeling blocked, in this Masterclass. I'm in self imposed isolation due to indirect exposure to Covid19. I'm ok, I don't feel sick, I have a place to live and we managed to get extra groceries, though now it's much more difficult. All the grocery delivery websites are crashed. I fluctuate between a) sadness because I can't see my daughter because she is in quarantine from exposure at work and b) livid anger at 'virus deniers' here who flaunt the Provincial state of emergency here. I'm thinking the only solution may be to bring in the army to forcefully disperse and arrest violators (crowds) – and I'm a Buddhist so that's an odd and strong thought for me.

So I'll push on by posting this and going back to David's videos. Maybe I'll start a topic called 'Writer's Block' cause I am an expert at it (at times)...

Social Distance Alarm Belt (blue tooth enabled, Alexa and Siri enabled on luxury model) (Spotify option)

Music : Say It Isn't So live at Daryl's House (Daryl Hall with guest Butch Walker)

or You Aint Going Nowhere by Perth County Conspiracy (written by Dylan when in self isolation)

Trigger alert : there is no fear of security but agoraphobics might not like this or maybe they will...

I'm always coming up with ideas for inventions. Usually while starring at the ocean view or usually when I can't sleep. John Lennon said he had a piano beside the bed so if he thought of a song in the night, he could play it a bit. If he forgot it by morning, it was no good. Me, if I remember my invention, I google it in the morning, only to discover it was patented 3 months before. This has happened with

- 'call your keys' (the lost app for misplaced keys)
- the cannabis CBD patch (like a nicotine patch but for good)
- a good recent one that is secret cause I forgot it but then remembered. I'll add it here somehow. (See bonus bandanas below)

But this one is patent pending, infomercial in production:

The Social Distancing Alarm Belt: 'the timely gift for yourself and loved ones'

Comes in stylish, fashion colours, you can change colour by app to match your Evening Wear (once the quarantine ends ...)

- the luxury one uses embedded lasers and is 5 G rated
- the discounted, now discontinued model used a radio frequency like in security alarms or bank tap debit cards.
- usb ready (handy in airports)
- silent or alarm mode
- ventilator friendly

It started as the concept of personal space. That area around you that feels uncomfortable, invasive if violated by someone. So this is why you need THE BELT that creates that magical 6 foot Social Distancing. All around your now safe being.

How it works (Laser Luxury Model):
8 lasers in all 8 directions sense any intrusion into your Social Distance and either alerts you personally by one of 64 signals to your phone/blue tooth or in a viral emergency, alerts a very large number of the crowd you don't want.
Note the colour options (app included) so your belt can blend in as anywhere from baby blue eye colour to flashing warning sign.
Optional : lasers can send out electric shocks to deter covidiots

Visit MySocialDistance.com for tech and payment details. Hurry as it's viral, trending and subject to hoarding.

BUT WAIT : Order in the next 24 hours and get your Mask Bandana. Yes, now you can quickly cover your mouth and nose when a 'virus denier' approaches. Each bandana comes with a choice of printed emojis or sayings such as 'Wash your fuckin Hands' ...

When I get rich with this invention, I'm buying a virus free island with state of the art security surrounding the island.

This was the last Assignment I did. I had bad writer's block made much worse by the asshole 'classmates' in the Masterclass who made idiotic comments. When I much later braved the audience to see David Sedaris live at a theatre, I should of said something to him when he asked the audience for questions. Like ' I read all your books Mr. Sedaris but your Masterclass really fucking sucks and I'd like my fucking money back.'

BONUS - Movie Reviews by Happy Pappy

I was asked by a new stoner (cannabis) magazine - never published due to Canadian laws - to write some short movie reviews. Not just stoner movies like *Cheech and Chong* but also cult movies that might scare you if stoned and alone...like psychological, not slashing shit...

I picked this one first. I almost picked *Harold and Maude* but this one is more obscure. Like remember when *Harold and Maude* was 'obscure' and I had to drive a great distance to see it at a theatre. Now TCM shows it fairly often and it's likely floating around on the net. However, it is very good film that really defines 'black comedy' so definitely a 'must see'.

Carnival of Souls (1962)

Written, produced, and directed by Herk Harvey (also uncredited as principal zombie)

Suggested music : She's Not There by the Zombies (Live on Hullabaloo TV Show, 1965)

Trigger alert : Those with kinemortophobia, fear of zombies or turning into a zombie, may want to stop reading or seek debriefing from possible terror flashbacks (this movie sticks with you...)

An independent film made with a budget of $33,000. The director used guerrilla film techniques such as filming quickly outside unknown to the public and innovative handheld camera shots.

This is another film that watching very late at night, alone and stoned is not recommended. The plot starts with 3 young women driving off a bridge while racing on a back road. The car is swept away but one of the women, Mary, mysteriously comes out of the water hours later. She has no recollection at all and moves to another city to play organ in a church. She proceeds to have visions of a zombie looking man. She finds that her reality comes and goes as at times there is no sound and she seems to be invisible to others. She becomes obsessed with an abandoned (zombie filled) carnival.

This film is not per se a zombie movie in the recent movie sense. The horror is really about the eerie organ soundtrack, her lapses with reality and her obsession. The director was inspired to use the actual abandoned carnival near Salt Lake City. The film was finished in 3 weeks and the director never made another film. Due to copyright problems, he never received any payments for the film. Candace Hilligoss who is excellent playing Mary, only appeared in one other film and 2 small one episode TV shows. However, she has a great website.

There are different edits/running times. The director's cut runs 84 minutes. It didn't get its deserved cult following as a low budget classic until the late 80s. The best DVD version is in the Criterion Collection and sells for around $30 on amazon. The black and white version (skip the colourized) is on youtube and appears to be the full length cut.

Being There, (1979)

Directed by Hal Ashby from the book by Jerzy Kosinski

I've got a rough list of films that I want to review. So I went through them to see if they were 'highly recommended stoned'. Without any problem, I found 3. There is also one ' extremely highly recommended must be stoned' but I'll save that one. *Being There*, *Crumb* (note it is unclear if I will review this as it would need a really big trigger alert/warning), and *Gods Must Be Crazy*.

I picked *Being There* (1979) because I was in a coffee shop and the barista and I somehow ended up mentioning *Being There* and they had never heard of it but quickly put it on their phone. Hipsterish move for sure. So I took that as a sign. Besides, I can't find my I Ching coins...

The plot surrounds Peter Sellers as a simple minded gardener for a wealthy man but he has never left the confines of this hidden courtyard in NYC. In dark hilarity, he is forced to leave when the man dies, ends up meeting wife of Mr. Rand who is a very powerful businessman. When he is taken to the Rand Mansion (actually the Biltmore mansion as a set), his name is confused as Chauncey Gardiner and his simple demeanour is interpreted as wisdom by Mr. Rand. The rest of the film basically takes place in the mansion. I don't want to say more as you must see the poignant hilarity.

Peter Seller's last film is nothing short of a triumph. He didn't win an Academy Award, and most certainly should have. Melvyn Douglas won best Supporting Actor. The film received glowing reviews and was very successful. I don't think I am giving a spoiler to say one of the famous lines is 'Life is a state of mind'. It was also Seller's epitaph when he died a year later.

This film now certainly rings a bell with the current political zeitgeist. Even without that, this film is on many lists of must see films.

Pappy says enjoy...

The Gods Must be Crazy (1980)

Written and directed by Jamie Uys

Bonus : Suggested Music - God Only Knows by The Beach Boys

A very funny movie, stoned or not. Though I'm on the preferred stoned side. Made for 10 million independently with all money raised locally, this film made 100 million world wide. I remember being at a cottage, 4 hour drive from Montreal, and this was having a North American premiere at a festival there and the reviews were so fantastic, I almost drove, not knowing that it would have worldwide distribution. It would be difficult to give spoilers for this film as right from the very start it is full of humour, sarcasm and slapstick. It all starts with a passing plane throwing out a coke bottle onto the San tribe in the Kalahari Desert. They live a simple, happy life in a very difficult place and believe that most things come from the Gods. Even this coke bottle. But because there is but one bottle, it creates dissension so Xi, played by non professional bushman actor N□xau who had never seen a camera of any kind before, is told to go to the edge of the world and throw it off so the Gods can take it back. He sets out with only the coke bottle and tranquilizing blow darts, his native language made up of click sounds. He proceeds to get into trouble and adventures with people he meets, a male researcher, a female teacher, a band of guerrillas who are chased by government troops and a cast of natives. His darts get him in trouble as well as save the day by capturing the guerrillas who have kidnapped the school children. Yet he remains true to his mission. It may not sound it, but the film is full of hilarity.

At the time of release, this film was regarded by some as racist though it is not blatant. What is true is that the natives never did get paid and N□xau was only paid $2000. After much controversy, he was paid $20,000. He was also in the sequel, not nearly as good a film.

Yet, the original film is hilarious and well worth a watch.

Pappy says enjoy.

The Harder They Come (1972)

Directed by Perry Henzell, music by Jimmy Cliff et al

Bonus : the famous, incredible reggae soundtrack by Jimmy Cliff, Toots and the Maytals and others

This Jamaican ganja crime film is credited with introducing much of the world to Reggae. The soundtrack is excellent Reggae. Again it is not hard to avoid spoilers as it wanders a little at points. It is fairly obvious that the budget wasn't great so the quality is not fantastic. However, all this only really adds to the film. It also has subtitles as the accent is so strong.

It was a huge hit in Jamaica likely because of its raw, realistic view of Kingston, Jamaica in the 60's. The soundtrack became popular, and now is considered an important cult film.

Jimmy Cliff is also the main character, Ivan. He moves from the country to Kingston as he dreams of becoming a reggae star. What he finds is stark poverty and hunger with no jobs. He does manage to record a song (title song) but is then introduced to the underworld through the record producer who is a gangster ganja dealer. Things do not go smoothly at all when he becomes a drug runner as eventually the gangster snitches on him to the police. Now he is desperate and on the run. The police are now after him. He escapes a few times by shooting his way out. As the film progresses he becomes more bold, seeing himself as a spaghetti western star.

Jimmy Cliff himself moved from the country to Kingston for school but as per the film found poverty but did not turn to crime. He recorded his first song at the remarkable age of 14. It became a hit in Jamaica. This film's soundtrack propelled him to worldwide attention. He still tours at age 71. He's released 31 albums and 51 compilation and best of albums as well as 92 singles !!! When you get a chance, listen to his music.
This film on youtube and has a Criterion DVD. In the original, pre-midnight show, unrated version, when Jimmy Cliff is lashed for slicing his antagonist, there are shots of frontal nudity when he is strapped over the barrel, making his urination explicit. The 25th Anniversary re-release cuts out the following scenes:

- The dinner with the Minister.
- Fixing the Bicycle.
- Part of the movie theatre scene where Ivan sees Jimmy Cagney stand off cops with empty guns.

Pappy says enjoy...

Dial M for Murder (1954)

Directed by Alfred Hitchcock

Bonus Suggested Music : Keeper of the Key by Perth County Conspiracy (dne)

SPOILER ALERT - this review is designed for people who have seen this film.

I won't really say much about the plot except about the apartment keys. The plot involves a husband arranging for a criminal to kill his wife and in Hitchcock style it goes all wrong. There is confusion over the door key. I have watched it at least 5 times before I 'think' I understand the key scenario which is the solution to the mystery.

For sake of ease, I will use character names : husband, wife, murderer, police inspector and the door key. You may want to use a diagram to follow what happens to the key or watch the movie a few times. This is what happens to the key (remember this is a spoiler alert) ;

1) husband shows murderer where the key will be hidden when he is to sneak into to kill wife

2) murderer uses the key but because of a delay in the plan returns the key but the door is still open

3) because wife kills murderer, husband has to scramble for new reasons to blame wife

4) husband removes key from now dead murderer and places in wife's purse. All unbeknownst by wife. Husband thinks this is the apartment key but as all apartment keys at the time look similar, he does not know that key was returned to hiding spot

5) husband still has his own key but the suspicious inspector switches keys with husband, unbeknownst to husband

6) now inspector arranges for husband to pick up purse of wife who is in prison falsely accused of murdering murderer

7) husband comes back expecting wife's key to work but it doesn't work in the door since the keys were switched

8) he realizes that real key is still in hiding place, uses it only to find inspector inside to arrest him

Confused? I still am about 5) and will need to watch once more and cheat with up to the minute key map/chart. Well worth the effort. Excellent film.

Pappy says enjoy.

Stroszek and the films of Werner Herzog

If you do not know Werner Herzog as a director, now is the time to discover his films.

I have picked his film *Stroszek* for a reason. A story to go along with it. When at university, I had a minor in film history with an emphasis on new wave foreign films. As a result, people in my other classes would ask me to recommend films. Of course, I looked at films from an often more technical/historical view and they didn't. Two people both complained to me that this film was way too depressing , never asked for another recommendation. Is this film depressing? Absolutely, very, fair warning, though it also can be seen as a very realistic view of parts of America. It is very bleak and the ending, though one of my favourite endings of a film, is certainly not a Hollywood ending as it is tragic but ever so memorable. All I will say is 'dancing chicken'...

It is not coincidental that Herzog himself had recently moved to the US. He wrote this film specifically for the main character, Strozek, who was played by Bruno S., a nonprofessional actor from Berlin. He was a street musician when Herzog cast him. Much of the film is based on Bruno S.'s real life though I don't think he really moved to the Midwest. Herzog referred to him as the best actor he had ever worked with, even though Bruno often had to talk rapidly for hours before doing any filming. You can very clearly see that this was possible and a perfect lead into the role.

This was no small claim by Herzog as he still is at it at age76. He has made 19 feature films, 7 shorts , 37 documentaries, acted in 25 films, and wrote every one of his films. An amazing career given that he had a difficult time breaking into film. Despite what my classmates said, it gets 100% on Rotten Tomatoes. Ok, ok – so it's bleak, very dark.

DVD $100 - $400, $3.99 on youtube watch, partly in German with subtitles.

This is Spinal Tap (1984)

Directed by Rob Reiner, written (music included) by Christopher Guest, Rob Reiner, Harry Shearer, Michael McKean
Supporting roles : Fred Willard, Fran Drescher

Bonus Suggested Music : from the soundtrack : Hell Hole (music video)

How to make a cult classic : get 60,000 $ for a script proposal, get 4 excellent musicians, comic actors together to work on a script, ad lib almost all the scenes with just a rough outline for each scene, make a 20 minute sample, find a budget of 2.5 million $ by shopping it to every studio, film dozens of hours, take almost no second takes (to keep it fresh), all in a 5 week shoot, edit to less than 2 hours, and make 250 million $. That's how. Oh I forgot. Rewrite the genre of documentary films with a brand new type. That helps too.

That's what happened with *This is Spinal Tap*. Despite receiving great reviews, it didn't initially do well at release. Perhaps because it was such a well done mockumentary, people didn't get it. In more than one instance, people told Christopher Guest that it would have been better film if he used a "better" band. Surely, the ultimate in compliments. Eventually, it caught on as a cult film once released on video.

It comes across as a real rockumentary. Right away, their pretentiousness is in your face just like their hilarious parody on heavy metal music. Some of the titles of the songs: *Hell Hole, Big Bottom, Sex Farm, Gimme Some Money*, give you a taste of how funny the songs are. The story involves the group's hopeful comeback tour of the US with record company hype but cancelled shows, small theatres and band drama. Every stop, every song, every incident is hilarious. It just must be watched.

Note there are different versions on DVD some with added deleted scenes. The Criterion DVD has the 20 minute initial sample.

youtube appears to have a complete free copy of the film. About $15 for DVD on amazon. Criterion DVD edition or the CD soundtrack are both worth about $500.

Pappy says enjoy.

www.ingramcontent.com/pod-product-compliance
Lightning Source LLC
LaVergne TN
LVHW041155150826
845673LV00001B/174

* 9 7 9 8 2 3 0 3 2 6 5 4 0 *